ABOVE THE FOLD

REVISED EDITION

ABOVE THE FOLD

Understanding the Principles of Successful Web Site Design

By Brian D. Miller

HOW BOOKS

For more excellent books and resources for designers, visit www.MyDesignShop.com.

18 17 16 15 14 5 4 3 2 1

ISBN-13: 978-1-4403-3666-9

Distributed in Canada by Fraser Direct
100 Armstrong Avenue
Georgetown, Ontario, Canada L7G 5S4
Tel: (905) 877-4411

Distributed in the U.K. and Europe by F&W Media International, LTD
Brunel House, Newton Abbot, TQ12 4PU, UK
Tel.: (+44) 1626-323200, Fax: (+44) 1626-323319
Email: enquiries@fwmedia.com
Distributed in Australia by Capricorn Link
P.O. Box 704, Windsor, NSW 2756 Australia
Tel.: (02) 44560-1600

Designed and art directed by Brian D. Miller
www.MillerSmith.com
@MillerSmithNews

Produced by Crescent Hill Books,
Louisville, KY
www.CrescentHillBooks.com

Every reasonable attempt has been made to identify owners of copyright. Errors or omissions will be corrected in subsequent editions.

For my two beautiful girls,
Sarah and Rachel

Acknowledgements

Thank you to my parents—the two most generous
souls I know.

Thanks to Alex White, mentor, colleague, and
plain ol' good friend.

Thank you to Nancy Heinonen for once again guiding
this process with patience and professionalism.

Thanks to my business partner Ian Smith.

Most of all, thank you to my family —Bridgette, Sarah
and Rachel. With love and gratitude this book is for you.

Table of Contents

Praise for Above the Fold First Edition

One of The Best Books Available On The Web Design Process
*Brian clearly put a lot of thought and careful consideration into
the structure, content and flow of the book. It's well done. I've been
building websites for 4 or 5 years now and this is the first book I've
found that does a good job of walking the reader through the entire
thought process of planning and creating a structured strategy for
designing websites."*
– Published on Amazon.com on April 28, 2011 by Steffan Antonas

Web Design Demystified
*"Above the Fold" provides everything that you need to build a strong
foundation for a successful web site."*
– Published on Amazon.com on March 28, 2011 by Ted A. Dobbs

I'm glad I started here
*Brian Miller gives a sensible and well thought out approach to web
design. As a person who is interested in getting into this field I found
this book a great place to begin my journey. He links all the steps to be
successful at web design. The talent and skills must be your own, but
if your looking for a tool to focus existing talent into a career in web
design this book is an excellent place to begin."*
– Published on Amazon.com on August 24, 2011 by JStein

Fantastic guide

Above the Fold provides you with the fundamentals required for a successful digital experience. Anyone who is looking to promote themselves or business using digital media marketing tools should own a copy of this book. As Brian Miller thoroughly demonstrates, principals of design very much apply to each of your digital properties. Thank you, Brian for an extremely comprehensive guide of an ever changing landscape. While technology will continue to change, principals of effective design do not."

– Published on Amazon.com on March 10, 2011 by B. Crosland

Great for budding Devs

If you're into the web and building sites then this, IMHO, is a must read. Brian Miller took his time and laid out the fundamentals of web development and design ehre in a concise and accessible manner. you don' need a lot of technical acumen or programming prowess to get what he's writing about and you'll come away with a much greater understanding of the how's and why's of dev/design."

– Published on Amazon.com on April 20, 2013 by Frater Zion

A Useful and Easy Guide

Miller has written here the perfect handbook for a student looking to learn more about web design or a small business owner trying to spice their site up an increase traffic. It's all here, discussions about the web itself, about how people use it and read different sorts of pages, discussions about the usability of a site and how that affects its design and vice-verse, a checklist of things to do before your site goes live and of things to have as it grows and thrives, everything you could need to know about web design."

– Published on Amazon.com on April 3, 2012
by A Student of eCommerce

A must have for web designers

Brian Miller does a great job of introducing people to the Art & Science of Website Design. This book is an excellent introduction and overview of Website Design, but is also packed with great information for old timers as well."

– Published on Amazon.com on September 11, 2011 by Hugh

Preface

For many years, students of graphic design studied the subject in the context of printed material (advertising, brochures, logos, books, magazines, newspapers, etc.) with the goal of creating a fixed and permanent product—ink on paper, paint on a wall. That is all changing. More recently, students studying graphic design do so with no intent of creating a piece of printed material. This book is for those students.

This book is also for those who have been practicing print design for many years and are looking to bridge their skills over to the Web. For you, there are portions of this book that should sound very familiar, but there will be other concepts that will go against what you've worked so hard to achieve as a print designer—letting go of exact color matching, smooth type rags, and avoiding the dreaded widow!

The fundamentals of clear, hierarchical graphic communication have not changed for hundreds, if not, thousands of years. There are universal principles that govern the success of a message being seen and being consumed effectively by a particular audience. But the medium matters. *Above the Fold* is a book about those enduring graphic design principles, but with the added nuances and specialties that digital communication brings.

This book focuses on the design of Web sites—more specifically, communicating a message using the medium of the Web. Many students of Web design, and many other publications on the topic, tend to mix technology (coding) and design into one big hodgepodge. This is a mistake and can be a barrier to entering the field for many people. Coding is an art form unto itself, requiring years of study and skill development, much like design. While it is important to understand the basics of the coding required to build a site, it is ambitious to believe that a single person will have the creative acumen to design a site as well as the coding prowess to develop the same site end to end.

This is very similar to print design, actually. It has always been important for graphic designers to understand the printing process—the effects of various types of varnishes or how certain paper affects the ink, folding, and binding techniques—but it has not been necessary for print designers to run the press. Although there are boutique print shops owned by very talented designers, the majority of pressmen are specialists in the field of printing. They understand that being an expert printer requires dedication, as does being a designer.

A few words about the title

Some of you may have investigated and/or purchased this book based on the title in the hope that it has the often-debated answer to the question, "Should I put all my content above the fold?" It is my hope that it will broaden your thinking on the subject. There is no one right answer to that question, but this book will provide you with the framework for effectively laying out a Web page based on the goals and objectives of your client.

The phrase **"above the fold"** reminds us that there are both close similarities and vast differences between print and Web design.

The term *above the fold* comes from the newspaper industry. There was a time when newspapers where sold en masse on the street corner to passersby. As people raced by from one location to another, the top of the front page of a newspaper needed to grab their attention and compel them to purchase the paper. In that case, it was very important to have the information on the top half of the front page be the most relevant and interesting.

For the Web, there is a similar paradigm where the viewable area of a Web browser only exposes a portion of most Web pages. The term *above the fold* was adopted by Web users to describe this phenomenon. Unlike newspapers, however, where almost every one was sold in a mass-market format, Web pages are viewed at different paces. Even pages within the same site are viewed differently—the home page tends to need to grab someone's attention faster than an interior page, as an example.

So why title the book *Above the Fold*? Good question. *Above the fold* is a phrase that reminds us that there are both close similarities and vast differences between designing for print and designing for the Web. It represents the link between what has been done for hundreds of years and what is new in the field of design.

Design can be defined as a series of decisions that lead to the optimal outcome for a particular need. Placing content above or below the fold on a Web page is one of those decisions. It is my hope that the content of this book will aid you in making this as well as many other important design decisions that lead to clear and effective communication on the Web.

INTRODUCTION TO WEB DESIGN

There's an old legend in the world of football that says Vince Lombardi, head coach of the Green Bay Packers, started every season with a speech to his players about the game of football. He began the lecture by holding up a football and saying, "Gentlemen, this is a football." He proceeded to describe its size and shape, talk about how it could be thrown, kicked, and carried. Then he'd point down at the field and say, "This is a football field." He'd walk around, describing the dimensions, the shape, the rules, and how the game was played.

This is the Internet

The message from the two-time Super Bowl-winning coach was simple: to truly be effective at anything, one can never forget the basics. This simple demonstration stripped away the complexities of the game and reduced it to its essence. In doing this, Mr. Lombardi refocused his team's attention on what was truly important about succeeding at the game of football.

Taking a cue from Vince Lombardi, I'd like to conduct a similar exercise for you: Turn on a Web-enabled device (PC, laptop, tablet, mobile phone, etc.), open the Web browser of your choice (Safari, Chrome, Firefox, Internet Explorer, etc.), type in the address of your favorite Web site, and behold—this is the Internet. The Internet is a series of interconnected computers, called servers, that enables companies, brands, organizations, governments, religious groups, and individuals to share information on a worldwide scale in real time. The World Wide Web, or Web, for short, is actually only a portion of the Internet, which also includes all aspects of computer-to-computer communication like email, messaging, and file serving, just to name a few.

When an Internet user types the address of a Web site into his or her Web browser, the device transmits a signal to a server, and the server responds by sending bits of information back to the computer. This information includes images, raw content, and instructions for the computer to reassemble the layout, called markup (the *M* in *HTML*). The computer then takes that information and configures the files based on two things: the markup and styles that came from the designer/developer, and the preferences and limitations of the Web browser and device itself. When a device reassembles a Web page that it has received from a server, the following factors influence exactly how that page appears on the screen.

CONNECTION SPEED

The connection speed is the speed with which a computer or device can connect to the Internet and download the assets required to build a page. This has been an on-again, off-again issue through the years. The first computers to connect to the Internet did so with modems that used phone lines, which were very slow, causing the need for "light-weight" pages—pages created mostly of text and color, with few images. Then came DSL and cable modems, making high-speed Internet possible, and Web page design evolved to include large amounts of imagery. Enter the cell phone, and people began browsing the Web with slower connection speeds, until Wi-Fi and high-speed mobile connections evolved. While the connection speed of a user browsing a site won't have a direct effect on how a site looks, it will definitely have an effect on the person's experience of the site.

SCREEN RESOLUTION

Not to be confused with the screen size in inches, resolution is the dimensions in pixels measured horizontally and vertically on a screen. Most desktop monitors range from 800 pixels wide by 600 pixels high to 1024 pixels wide by 768 pixels high. Tablets have similar resolutions, while mobile devices can be as little as 320 pixels wide. Because of this dilemma of differing screen resolutions, designers and developers created the idea of responsive design. Discussed further in chapter 3, responsive design displays different layouts for a single Web page in response to the screen resolution, making it possible to maximize legibility and usability regardless of the size of the screen the content is displayed on.

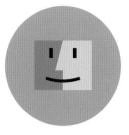

OPERATING SYSTEM

The type of device and version of the operating system (OS) the audience is using to browse a site can have an effect on how a site is seen. The number of operating systems has increased over recent years. Instead of focusing on Macintosh versus Microsoft Windows, designers and developers now have mobile platforms to contend with— iOS (Apple), Windows Mobile, Android (Google) and to some extent Blackberry. A primary difference between operating systems is how typography is handled, including the fonts that are available natively and how smoothly the fonts are rendered. Chapter 6 takes an in-depth look at typography.

WEB BROWSER

The primary Web browsers used today are Safari, Chrome, Firefox, and Internet Explorer, both desktop and mobile versions. A Web browser is an application whose function is to receive layout and styling information from a host and display that information on screen. Because these are different applications developed by different companies, they all interpret this information slightly differently. Added to this, the language that makes up Web styling—cascading style sheets, or CSS—is always evolving; therefore, Web browsers are constantly updating to keep up with the latest styling attributes.

Designing for the Web

To complicate matters, beyond these inherent system-based influences, individual user preferences also can affect the way a site looks. In this image we see the "Content" preferences in the Firefox Web browser. These controls allow a savvy Web user to change the fonts, the minimum size for type (this is an accessibility feature for users with impaired vision), the colors used for links, and even whether links are underlined. In some cases, these user preferences can even override the design decisions a designer has made for a page.

It is this aspect of disassembling a design and allowing the user to reassemble it under a varying set of circumstances that makes Web design a unique and challenging form of design. These unique factors create added limitation considerations, and new possibilities, for the designer. Dealing with these factors and the potential issues they can cause in the clear communication of a message or a brand image requires a specific process.

This screenshot of the preferences panel in Firefox shows how users can change how specific characteristics of Web design appear on their screen.

Limiting **subjective decisions** and being creative within those limitations is the essence of what all designers do.

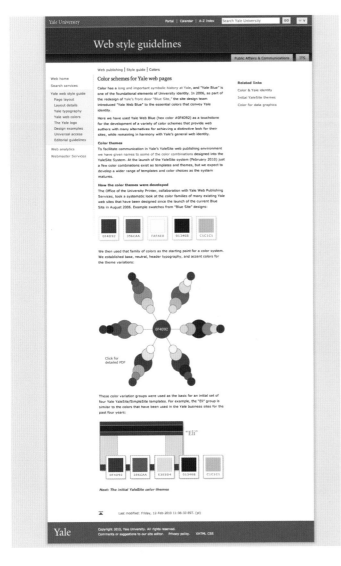

The influence of the Web browser on Web design can be seen clearly in the following timeline. As the browser evolved, so did the sophistication of the design treatments for Web pages. Also evident on the following timeline is the uniquely Web idea of "publish, then polish." For many Web-based organizations, like the ones in the timeline, getting something online is more important than getting the perfect thing online. This can be very counterintuitive for print designers, who are used to meticulous perfection prior to any public consumption.

Most organizations have Web standards like this one for Yale. They spell out the dos and don'ts of everything from typography and color to image use and grid structure. These rules help define the creative decisions made by a Web designer and ensure brand consistency.

11

A Brief History of Web Design

Web 1.0 (1993 – 2002)

Mosaic, the first consumer Web-browsing application, is released

Image of Microsoft.com from 1994

WC3 is formed to standardize HTML

Netscape Navigator Web browser is released

Yahoo.com launches

Amazon.com launches

NYTimes.com launches

CraigsList.org launches

Microsoft releases Internet Explorer versions 1 (August) and 2 (November)

CompuServe changes its name to Lycos.com

Cascading style sheets (CSS) introduced

Microsoft releases Internet Explorer version 4

DrudgeReport.com launches

Image of Apple.com from 1997

Ebay.com launches

Netscape Communicator replaces Netscape Navigator

1993   **1994**   **1995**   **1996**   **1997**

Google.com, founded by Larry Page and Sergey Brin, launches

Napster.com, a peer-to-peer file sharing Web site, launches

Microsoft releases Internet Explorer version 5, which allowed users to save Web pages for the first time

Craigslist.org expands beyond San Francisco (originally launched in 1995)

Google Adwords launches

Netscape version 6 is released

Wikipedia.org launches

Microsoft releases Internet Explorer version 6, which included support for CSS

Friendster.com launches

Netscape version 7 is released

1998   **1999**   **2000**   **2001**   **2002**

A Brief History of Web Design

Web 2.0 (2003 – present)

MySpace.com launches

WordPress blogging software is introduced.

Apple releases the Safari Web browser

Facebook.com launches

Flickr.com launches

Mozilla Firefox Web browser is released, which utilizes the Gecko layout engine to display Web pages

YouTube.com launches

Twitter.com launches

Microsoft releases Internet Explorer version 7, which introduced tabbed browsing and a content feed reader

Mozilla Firefox version 2 is released with tabbed browsing

Apple introduces the iPhone and mobile apps

Netscape Navigator version 9 is released

2003　　**2004**　　**2005**　　**2006**　　**2007**

Candidate Web sites and social media play a pivotal role in the U.S. elections

Mozilla Firefox version 3 is released

Microsoft launches Bing.com to compete with Google

Microsoft releases Internet Explorer version 8 with improved support for Ajax, CSS, and RSS

Twitter.com is used to organize and mobilize relief efforts in Haiti following the devastating earthquake.

Mozilla Firefox version 3.6 is released

Pinterest.com launches

Vine.com launches

2008   2009   2010   2011   2012

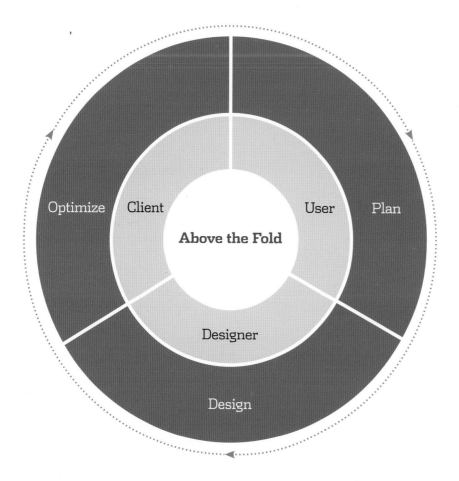

Above the Fold *focuses on the three phases of a Web project—planning, designing, and optimizing—with each phase aligning with the constituents of a Web site: the user, the designer, and the client.*

Plan

The first section of *Above the Fold* explores the steps that are required to plan out a Web site. Planning is not unique to Web design, of course, but there are some unique considerations a Web designer must be aware of in order to avoid common pitfalls. Even the simplest of Web sites can be defined as an application with a unique set of utilities that need to be manipulated by the user. Identifying the requirements of this application, including the goals of the client, is a great first step for any Web project. The resulting requirements document can be referred to throughout the entire project to create success factors to be used to evaluate the project in the end.

Another benefit of this planning stage is that it helps designers break up large tasks into manageable smaller tasks. Mapping out the relationships between large amounts of complex information or detailing the flow of a particular user task are examples of things that should be addressed prior to beginning the design phase in order to make sure they're getting the attention they require.

In addition to having a plan, Web designers need to have a contingency plan—a backup plan that allows for user variables.

The collection of these plans is called User Experience Design, or UX. Designing the experience that's right for the target customer (in addition to what we traditionally think of as graphic design—styling, typography, and imagery) is critical to being a successful Web designer. It's the criteria by which each of the samples shown in this book has been judged. They go beyond looking good: they look good, they work well, and in many cases they add an element of delight to the experience. It's also the criteria that the Web-browsing population uses to determine how successful a Web site will be.

Take twitter.com, for example. It's unlikely to win a traditional design award, yet it's undeniably and profoundly popular. Twitter's popularity is largely due to two main things: It's a simple idea—telling your friends what you're up to—executed simply, with an emphasis on user interaction. It is a utility that lets users have enough control over the experience to make them feel as if they're expressing themselves, but not so much control that the experience becomes overwhelming or intimidating. This is all a direct result of excellent planning and user experience design.

Design

The second section of *Above the Fold* looks at the specific attributes of Web design and layout. To explore the subject of design for any medium, it's important to define the term *design*. At its most basic, design is a plan. Things that are said to have happened "by design" are said to have happened not by accident.

A finished design is simply the result of a series of decisions made by a designer to uphold a specific brand image and communicate a message. Each decision a designer makes leaves him or her open for subjective criticism, and therefore, many designers find it helpful if their decision set is limited in some way—by brand guidelines, client requests, or self-imposed limits. Limiting subjective decisions and being creative within those limitations is the essence of what all designers do.

The Web as a design medium comes with several built-in design decision limitations—from color accuracy to typographic control to page size. Successful Web designers embrace these limitations and find ways to be creative within them, instead of trying to circumvent them. Section II of *Above the Fold* explores the aspects of graphic design (space use, typography, imagery) in the context of the limitations and opportunities that Web design offers.

Design is about having a plan. Web design is about having a **backup plan.**

Optimize

The final step in the Web design process, as well as the last section of *Above the Fold*, is the analysis phase. Analysis can begin with the product itself—the Web site that was created in the design phase. This testing, or beta, stage can help uncover issues with the digital product prior to launching the site to the public.

Once the site is launched, how will your users find it? Section III looks at two ways of attracting visitors: search engine optimization (SEO) and Web marketing. SEO is not a sexy topic. It involves research, copywriting, and networking. But it is paramount to the success of a site. Marketing is very sexy—social, viral, guerrilla. It is these concepts of SEO and marketing that bring users to a site and ultimately lead to its business success.

Finally, Web design offers an unprecedented opportunity to analyze and adjust a design based on detailed, real-time information. Improvements to the design or usability of a site can be done on the fly with no limits to the number of changes that can be made. Analytic software, such as Google Analytics, provides countless pieces of data that help a designer understand the habits of the users of a site.

Each of the topics in *Above the Fold*, from planning and design to marketing and analysis, can be researched in much greater depth than what is presented here. It is also equally important to take in the breadth of these principles. They are interconnected; too great a focus on one area over another will result in a less than successful product. Planning, designing, analyzing, and back again to planning is the complete and necessary cycle for successful and long-lasting Web strategies.

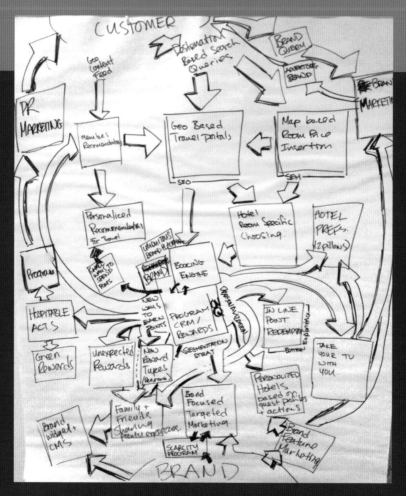

Illustration by Bryan Hamilton

Section I

PLAN

CHAPTER 1

WEB SITE PLANNING

User-focused design, or design that puts the user ahead of stylistic design treatments or gratuitous use of technology, must start with a plan. The objective of this plan is to align the client's business goals with the needs and desires of the target user group. A plan can also help map out a "big picture" view of the project, giving all members of the team perspective, clarity, and a common goal. An effective plan helps remove subjectivity from the creative process and gives a framework for decision-making.

Project Planning

Creating a Web site project plan is a multi-part, multi-disciplinary process. The phases of this process can include research and discovery, content inventory, site mapping, wireframing, usability mapping, prototyping, and design concepting, all of which are discussed in this chapter. Depending on the size of the project, this phase can take a week to several months to establish the documents needed to effectively move forward with the design phase.

There are many benefits to developing an effective site plan. The client should reap long-term benefits, from a reduction in the development cost normally associated with inflexible or flawed systems, to decreased training costs. These benefits help clients make the most of their Web site and achieve the highest return on their investment (ROI).

Plans also help the design team define the parameters of a project for estimating purposes. Once a plan is in place, the designer or project team should have a clear picture of the scope of work (SOW) for the project. The team can then estimate and assign time to each task or phase of the project. If along the way the client has revisions or changes direction, the designer or project team can refer back to the approved plan and determine whether the project needs to be re-estimated or if the alterations are within the original scope of work.

Ultimately, however, site planning should be about the user. The goal of a well-conceived site plan is to increase a user's satisfaction with a site by organizing information and optimizing the critical tasks on the site. The measure of the ease of use for a site is called usability and is discussed in the next chapter. What follows are the basic steps involved in the Web site planning stage.

Research & Discovery

The process of developing a plan usually starts with research into the client's goals for the site and an analysis of the landscape in which a site will exist. A briefing meeting is an interview with the client to better understand the purpose behind the project. This can be conducted by a designer or an account executive (also called a client manager), whose job is to manage the client relationship. A SWOT (strengths, weaknesses, opportunities, and threats) analysis can be very helpful in pinpointing the internal and external factors that will influence the project. A SWOT analysis categorizes the internal and external, positive and negative factors that can influence the effectiveness of a site.

To gain a deeper understanding of the landscape, it's often necessary to conduct a competitive analysis and customer interviews. A competitive analysis results in noting what the competition does well as well as where they fall short. This can help identify gaps in the market that the client can take advantage of. Customer interviews are helpful for identifying the current perception of the client organization or the general feeling of the current market.

The result of a client briefing and customer interviews is a project or creative brief. A creative brief outlines the goals for a project, the special considerations the team must take in order to complete the project effectively, as well as a schedule of milestone events. A brief is usually reviewed by the team and the client and signed off, forming the directional foundation for the project.

To the right is an example of a SWOT analysis. The process of developing a SWOT chart can help uncover key pieces of information that help shape the usability and concept of a Web site. Strengths and weaknesses are internal factors, while opportunities and threats are external factors that a client has little control over.

A **SWOT analysis** categorizes the internal
and external, positive and negative factors
that can influence the effectiveness of a site.

Strengths
Internal/Positive

Recognized brand

Impressive product line

Weaknesses
Internal/Negative

Understaffed

Lack of experience

Opportunities
External/Positive

Expanding customer base

Growing industry

Threats
External/Negative

Strong competition

Economic factors

Requirements Documentation

A great way to organize the client's needs and create a list of success factors is with a requirements document. A requirements document is usually a spreadsheet that contains a list of non-subjective "must-haves" for each page or section of a site as well as global must-haves for the whole site. An example of a requirement is "the site shall have commerce functionality," or "the main navigation shall include a link to the shopping cart feature." These requirements help set a framework for the rest of the planning stage and they can be referred to throughout the project to ensure the success of the project.

(Opposite) This creative brief template helps clients synthesize the goals of a project in a way that can help remove a lot of the subjectivity that comes with creative projects.

(Below) A Gantt chart shows the timing of the tasks involved in a project in relationship to one another, helping the team see the big picture.

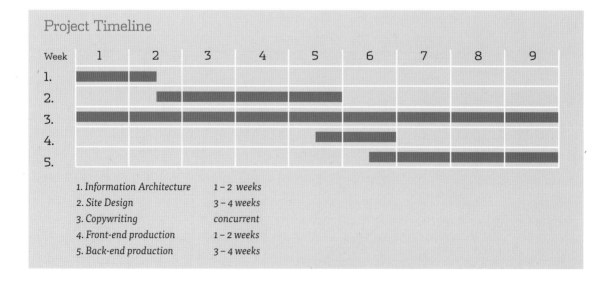

Project Timeline

Week	1	2	3	4	5	6	7	8	9
1.									
2.									
3.									
4.									
5.									

1. *Information Architecture*   1–2 *weeks*
2. *Site Design*   3–4 *weeks*
3. *Copywriting*   *concurrent*
4. *Front-end production*   1–2 *weeks*
5. *Back-end production*   3–4 *weeks*

Creative Brief

Project name:

Date:

Prepared by:

Submitted to:

Project overview:

Background information:

Target user insight information:

Brand attributes, promise, and mission:

Competitive landscape:

Business objectives—success criteria:

Testing requirements—measurement of success:

Creative strategies:

Functionality and technical specifications:

Contribution and approval process:

Timelines:

Budget:

This fact-based portion of the brief should be concise and only include information pertaining to the desired outcome of this specific project

The business objective should identify a single testing metric that drives the creative strategy and the decision-making process for the project

Defining the number of rounds of revisions and identifying a single point of contact (client and creative) will cause clients to focus their comments and streamline the process

Asset Inventory

A Web site design project can often be overwhelming at the beginning. There are many considerations to be made and items to be collected before designing can begin. Project assets like client logos, copywriting, imagery, and code libraries must all be identified and located. This process begins with an inventory of all the assets needed for a project—in other words, what are the elements of a site that the team will need to complete the project? This information can be collected in a spreadsheet, drawn out on a whiteboard, or sorted on index cards—whatever will produce the most comprehensive results. This process can be done by the creative team in parallel with the execution of other phases by the information architecture and user experience teams.

Content Checklist

Copy

☐ Who will provide copy?

☐ Is there a budget for a copywriter?

☐ What are the copy mandatories?

☐ What's the correct tone for the audience and brand?

Imagery & Artwork

☐ Is there existing imagery?
   If yes, what format and resolution is it?

☐ Is there a budget for a photo shoot?

☐ Is there a stock photo budget?

☐ Are any custom illustrations needed?

Code

☐ What code can be reused, if any?

☐ Does this require custom programming or an off-the-shelf solution?

☐ Will there be a content management system (CMS)?

☐ Who will manage the content?

File Organization & Naming

A designer's ability to organize his or her working and production files is always important, but with Web design it's critical. This is because the files that a designer uses to create a site are the same files that a user will download and view on his or her computer. Factors such as file name, file type, file size, and directory organization are all significantly more important than with print design. HTML files reference other files with relative paths, which means they find other files based on their own location. Therefore, files need to be organized in clearly labeled directories, as seen in the diagram to the right.

Properly naming files can help improve workflow and, more importantly, ensure the files will be handled properly by the Web server. Rule number one is never use spaces in file names. While Mac and Windows systems can handle spaces with no issue, servers running UNIX can have difficulty with spaces.

Clear file names help the programmer understand the content of the file and they help organize the directories for a Web site. The example file names seen here are all buttons, thus they start with "btn_" and because of this they group together alphabetically. Note that they're all lowercase as well. This is for consistency and because some languages like XML and XHTML are case sensitive, so to be safe designers should stick with an all-lowercase convention.

Main Directory

HTML/CSS files

Image directory

Javascript directory

Media directory

btn_red.gif
btn_blue.gif
btn_green.gif
btn_orange.gif

Taxonomy and Grouping

Once the objectives have been set and all of the things the client would like to say and do with the site have been established, you can begin organizing and mapping out the content. Start by listing all the content. Then begin grouping the content logically. "Logically" can mean a number of things—logically from a business point of view or how the client sees things being grouped, or logically from a user's point of view or how the information will be consumed.

Some Information Architects (IAs) conduct this exercise with software like OmniGraffle, or the old-fashioned way, with index cards. How you decide to do this is up to you, but the ultimate solution should be something that makes sense for the user and the client.

One rule of thumb is to limit the number of choices a user sees at any given point to seven items. Physiologically, humans cannot perceive more than seven items at one time without creating sub-groups. So to not overwhelm the user, a typical primary navigation will not have more than seven items, often fewer.

Hierarchy of information can begin to unfold with the selections for the primary and secondary navigations. The primary navigation should be just that, the primary activities that a user will want to conduct on the site. The secondary navigation, which often has less visual importance, is for supporting content.

On a side note, I can't tell you how many times I have clients request that "About Us" appear in the main navigation. One of the hardest jobs of an information architect is getting clients to understand the point of view of the user. "I'm sorry to say it, Mr. Client, but users don't care about you." Or at least, it's not their primary concern. "Yes, it's nice to hear how you worked for years to develop your product or service and how you started in your basement, but that is not why people are visiting your site..."

Information Architecture

In order to understand what information architecture (also known as IA) is, it's important to unlearn what most designers think IA is. It is a mistake to think of IA as simply a means of sketching a design—boxes and shapes that represent the "underpainting" of a layout. While this may be useful to some designers and may also be how IA got its start, it's only a sliver of the IA field, which extends well beyond simple design planning.

In the infancy of the Internet, Web sites were predominantly "information spaces"—news sites, medical sites, marketing brochure sites, etc. Therefore, there was a need to "architect" these spaces, which meant designing effective ways to a) organize the content, and b) navigate through it so users could easily find what they were looking for. If you look at the deliverables an information architect (also known as an IA) created, that becomes clear, below.

 Site maps: An illustration or map of the pages of a site and their relationship to one another

 Taxonomies: The classification of content into a hierarchical structure

 Labeling systems: The process of naming buttons and links to make it clear what content they will reveal

 Wireframes: A means of organizing the content of an individual page as well as illustrating any technical requirements needed

These tools illustrate the navigation structure and provide context as well as the details of the various information components shared across the different pages/screens of the site.

When websites became more transactional, IAs started to become more like interaction designers, thinking in terms of discrete user tasks, mapping out user flows, designing—from a functional point of view—the individual components that would allow users to complete tasks, and all the nitty-gritty that went into each component. At this point, IAs shifted their attention away from the client and/or the designer and focused it squarely on the user. User scenarios became a standard IA deliverable, showing the paths to desired user outcomes and (usually) business outcomes, too.

Sitemap

The information architecture phase of a Web site project starts with the development of a comprehensive sitemap. A sitemap is a schematic for a site showing the pages and the linked relationships among them. Traditionally, pages are represented by outlined boxes, and links are represented by lines connecting the boxes. This document gives a design team an overview of the site and allows designers to understand the breadth of the navigational needs and the full scope of the project: What pages are most important? What pages need to be reached from every page? Is there a target page that the client wants to lead people to? All of these questions can be answered by examining a sitemap.

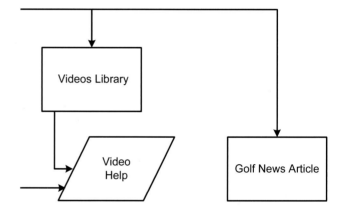

A sitemap, like the one shown here for GolfersMD.com, shows the pages of a site and their relationship to one another. Pages are laid out and grouped by the information architect, showing various pathways and connections that a design team uses when laying out the navigation and sub-navigation. In this case, the items in the main navigation are shaded in blue, pages that require the user to log in are shaded in gray, and pop-up windows are slanted boxes.

The sitemap on the next page illustrates that even a very large and seemingly unwieldy site becomes more manageable when neatly organized by an information architect.

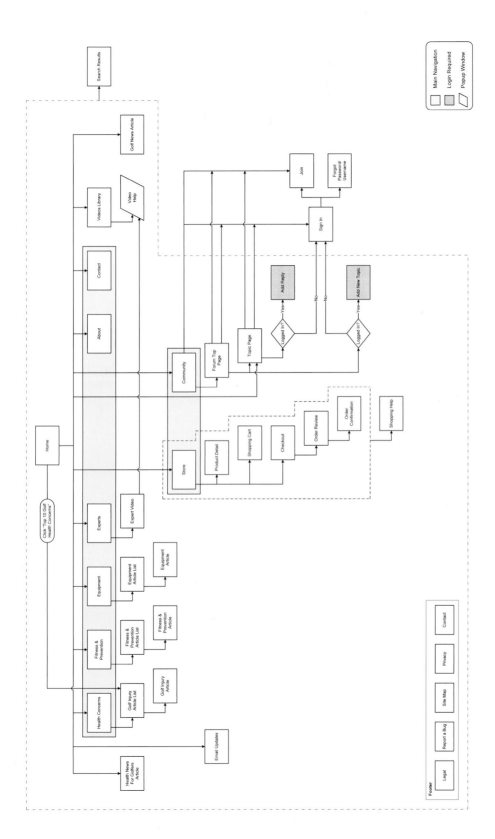

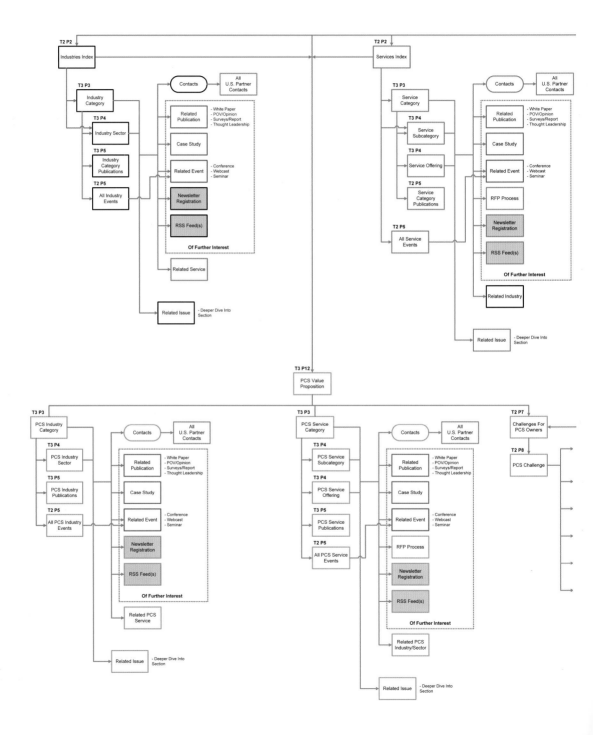

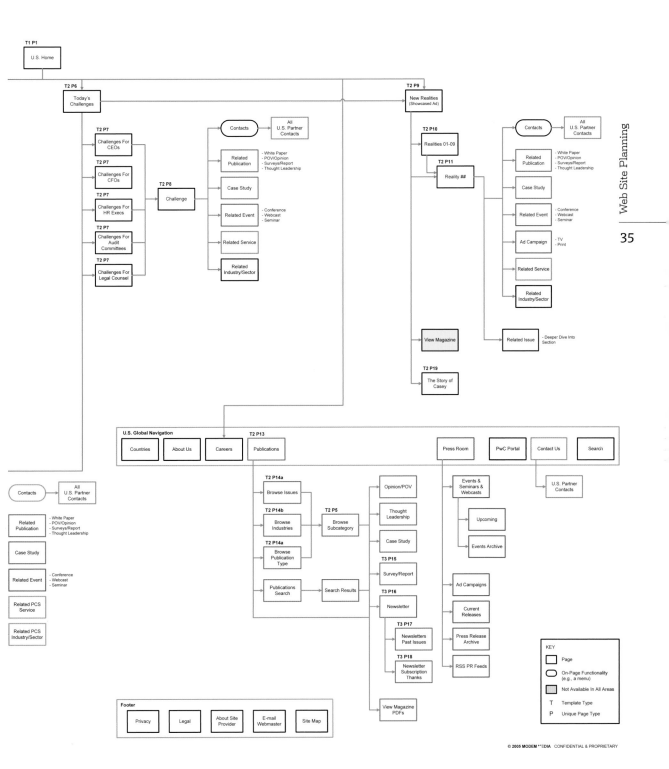

Web Site Planning

35

T1 P1 — U.S. Home

T2 P6 — Today's Challenges

T2 P7 — Challenges For CEOs
T2 P7 — Challenges For CFOs
T2 P7 — Challenges For HR Execs
T2 P7 — Challenges For Audit Committees
T2 P7 — Challenges For Legal Counsel

T2 P8 — Challenge

Contacts
All U.S. Partner Contacts

Related Publication
- White Paper
- POV/Opinion
- Surveys/Report
- Thought Leadership

Case Study

Related Event
- Conference
- Webcast
- Seminar

Related Service

Related Industry/Sector

T2 P9 — New Realities (Showcased Ad)

T2 P10 — Realities 01-09

T2 P11 — Reality ##

Contacts
All U.S. Partner Contacts

Related Publication
- White Paper
- POV/Opinion
- Surveys/Report
- Thought Leadership

Case Study

Related Event
- Conference
- Webcast
- Seminar

Ad Campaign
- TV
- Print

Related Service

Related Industry/Sector

View Magazine

Related Issue
- Deeper Dive Into Section

T2 P19 — The Story of Casey

U.S. Global Navigation

Countries | About Us | Careers | **T2 P13** Publications | Press Room | PwC Portal | Contact Us | Search

U.S. Partner Contacts

T2 P14a — Browse Issues
T2 P14b — Browse Industries
T2 P14a — Browse Publication Type
Publications Search

T2 P5 — Browse Subcategory

Search Results

Opinion/POV
Thought Leadership
Case Study
T3 P15 — Survey/Report
T3 P16 — Newsletter
T3 P17 — Newsletters Past Issues
T3 P18 — Newsletter Subscription Thanks

View Magazine PDFs

Events & Seminars & Webcasts
Upcoming
Events Archive
Ad Campaigns
Current Releases
Press Release Archive
RSS PR Feeds

Contacts
All U.S. Partner Contacts

Related Publication
- White Paper
- POV/Opinion
- Surveys/Report
- Thought Leadership

Case Study

Related Event
- Conference
- Webcast
- Seminar

Related PCS Service

Related PCS Industry/Sector

Footer

Privacy | Legal | About Site Provider | E-mail Webmaster | Site Map

KEY

☐ Page
◯ On-Page Functionality (e.g., a menu)
▨ Not Available In All Areas
T Template Type
P Unique Page Type

Wireframes are **blueprints** that map out individual pages of a site. They show the elements of a page and their relative weight or importance.

Wireframe

Wireframes are blueprints that map out individual pages. The wireframe shows the elements of a page and their relative weight or importance. They are not intended to illustrate the layout of the page; instead, they visually catalog the elements on a page and give a designer an idea of what the most important elements are, what the second most important elements are, and so on. They can also detail specific functionality for a page; illustrate different states for elements on the page or the entire page, like drop-down menus or expanding areas; or demonstrate how modular areas might work together.

Wireframes can be made for any page of the site that requires this type of detail, like the home page, subpage templates, registration forms, search results, and so on. This step helps a designer focus on style rather than a dual task of form and function during the layout phase.

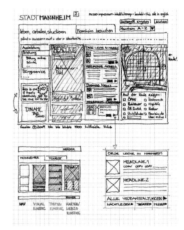

The wireframes seen here and on the next spread are what user experience experts and information architects use to organize a page for a design team. Wireframes are the bones that a designer uses to flesh out by adding brand elements and aesthetic treatments.

| Logo | _SITE NAME_ | | Welcome, Swhite | Settings | Help | Logout |

Tuesday, February 20, 2007   Find a Colleague ▽ | Browse By Tag ▽ | [   ] [Search]

| Home | Blog | Prof. Development | Knowledge Resources | Marketing Excellence | My Profile

---

In The Spotlight

Nike to Change Shopping Experience

Nike wants to change the way consumers shop!

"Consumers want a more compelling and relevant experience wherever and whenever they shop," Nike President and Chief Executive Mark Parker said.

Discuss on the Blog >

Latest Blog Post

Sterling Hayden on Feb 20, 2007:

Integer consequat. Sed sed lacus. Aliquam erat volutpat. Pellentesque facilisis urna quis odio. Curabitur rhoncus.

Aliquam erat. Donec at libero vel mi dignissim accumsan. Nam ante tellus, porta ut, sollicitudin id. Nullam fermentum luctus leo...

Go To Post >

Featured Content

Campaigns   Knowledge Base

5th Anniversary of Volvo's awards program honoring America's favorite hometown heroes.

Campaign: "Volvo For Life"
Media: TV, Online, Print, Event

Go To Campaign >

| News | Clip Sheets | Select Feeds ▽

News: All Topics   Search News ▽

Most Recent | Most Viewed | Top Rated | All Stories

- **10 Secrets of Successful Online Community**
  Tue Feb 20, 2007 02:37 PM (_SOURCE_)
  Views: 128,234 ☆☆☆☆☆ Avg. Rating (0 votes) Tags: _TAG NAME_, _TAG NAME_

- **The Ultimate Social Network You Haven't Heard Of**
  Tue Feb 20, 2007 01:54 PM (_SOURCE_)
  Views: 536 ★★★☆☆ Avg. Rating (498 votes) Tags: _TAG NAME_

- **Hyundai QarmaQ's Plastic Skin: Reduces Weight, Saves Gas**
  Tue Feb 20, 2007 01:20 PM (_SOURCE_)
  Views: 413 ★★★★★ Avg. Rating (405 votes) Tags: _TAG NAME_, _TAG NAME_

- **Google Shifting Resources to YouTube Monetization**
  Tue Feb 20, 2007 11:09 AM (_SOURCE_)
  Views: 402 ★★★☆☆ Avg. Rating (233 votes) Tags: Not Tagged

- **Sharing is saving: GM to save up to $750 million on Zeta RWD platform**
  Tue Feb 20, 2007 11:02 AM (_SOURCE_)
  Views: 8 ★★★★☆ Avg. Rating (8 votes) Tags: _TAG NAME_, _TAG NAME_ ◄

[<< Previous] [1] [2] [3] [4] [5] [6] [7] [8] [9] [10] ... [63] [64] [Next >>]

Appears on rollover of link (see CoolIris.com). Click to open article in layer as shown on next wireframe.

BuzzMetrics Stats

Brand: [Volvo   ▽]

Total identified blogs: **42,192,419**

New blogs in last 24 hours: **66,477**

Blog posts indexed in last 24 hours: **503,650**

Go To Report >

Events Calendar

| 04-04-2007 | Ford Marketing Conference | New York, NY USA |
| 04-24-2007 | Advertising Age: Marketing In The Digital Age | London, England UK |

See Full Calendar >

Suggestions For The Site?

Have some great content and feature ideas for the site? Discuss them in the Site Suggestions blog.

If there is a premium on space and a desire to display more headlines above the fold, consider NOT showing the "Views, Rating, Tag" line. The values are implicit in the filtering choices on the top bar and via the Tags option in the Search News dropdown. They are also explicitly displayed when the article is opened.

Usability Diagrams

Usability diagrams (also known as user-flow diagrams or use cases) combine a sitemap and a wireframe to plan out a specific action a user might take on a site, and the process of how it occurs. Each step of a process is illustrated especially for tasks that have multiple outcomes, like error and success messages. For example, to show how someone might register as a user on a site, a usability diagram would show a home page, a registration page that's linked from the home page, an error page showing that the user didn't complete all the required fields, a "thank you" page showing the registration was complete, and a confirmation email wireframe. User-flow diagrams show every step of the process and can help uncover potential issues. The process of creating a use case can be as valuable as the resulting diagram. The exercise of acting as a user and imagining interaction with the site is a critical preparation step in designing for the Web.

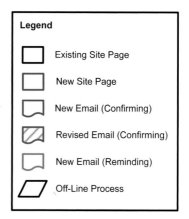

The usability diagram seen here goes a step beyond a sitemap and illustrates the path a user might take through a site. The diagram can include not only on-site pages, but emails and even off-site actions like going to a retail store or calling an 800 number. These help the Web project team lead the user to the intended goal of the client in the most effective way.

On-Boarding Flow

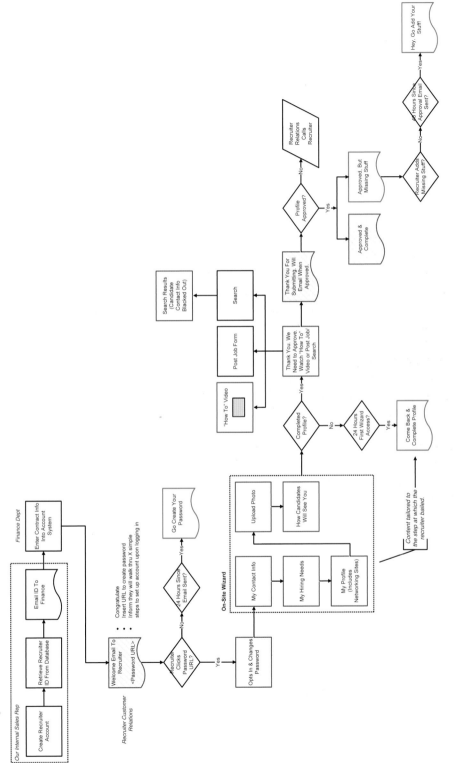

Prototypes are working models of site functionality that help a developer work out the final details and provide **proof of concept.**

Prototypes

Once the wireframing is complete and critical tasks are mapped out, it's sometimes necessary to create functional prototypes for new or complicated functionality. Prototypes are working models of site features or functionality that help a developer and a designer work out the final details and provide proof of concept. These working models, which are usually void of any design treatment, provide valuable opportunities for evaluation and refinement that can't be done with diagrams alone. Once a prototype is functional, it's ready to be "skinned" by the designer. Skinning is a term used by designers that means to add a design treatment on top of a working model.

Prototypes, like the ones seen here, are created by the development team to flesh out specific technological challenges and to create a proof of concept that an idea can actually be executed.

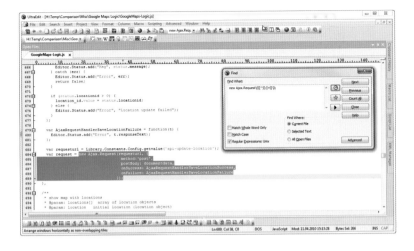

Functionality development can take a lot of trial and error before it's ready for deployment. This back-and-forth process can often yield valuable testing data that can help both the design and usability teams.

Concept Design: Mood Boards

The beginning creative stages of a Web design project are not unlike other creative projects. They involve understanding the goals of the client, understanding the audience, and creating a vision for how those two ideas can meet—and of course, how the designer can express creativity and originality in the process.

One way that designers begin the creative process is to gather and collect visual samples that relate to the visual feel or brand image for a specific project. These visual samples, or swipe, can come from anywhere—sites like Pinterest.com are a great place to start, but designers also pull from physical magazines and catalogs, Google image searches, and by taking their own photography. The swipe collected for a mood board can include:

Imagery: Finding the right imagery style for a project can help the designer understand the creative direction.

Iconography: Iconography styles vary widely. A mood board should present a single, consistent style.

Color: Having a color theme for a project is important for providing visual unity and setting a tone or mood.

Texture: Often overlooked, texture can bring a concept to life and add a richness that sets a design apart.

Typography: Type plays a critical role in any design and should therefore be carefully considered in relation to the other design elements.

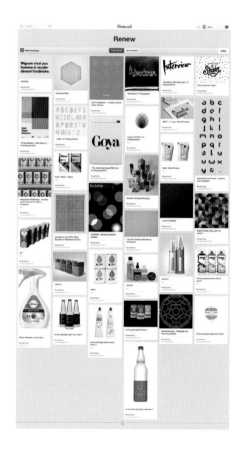

Seen above is a Pinterest.com board of type, imagery, illustration, which will serve as inspiration for a design project. Pinterest is a great way to quickly collect and organize elements of a mood board.

The mood boards seen here and on the next page were created by the Wonderfactory to help their client get a feel for the visual mood of a site prior to seeing the finished design, also shown here.

To create an effective mood board, designers start by grabbing as many appealing samples of these elements as they can find, collecting them in cohesive groups. Telling a story is a big part of this exercise, but simply grouping elements based on the story they tell isn't enough; there must be visual unity. Once you have a visual story with several images, colors, texture, and typography, codify them onto what is known as a mood board.

Mood boards help you and the client understand the overall look of a site without getting bogged down with the details of navigation or other details of a Web site. The loose feel lets clients use their imagination—with a little help from you, of course. Most of all, a mood board is meant to garner an emotional response from the client—"I love it!" In addition to helping your client understand your vision for a site, a mood board can also help you brief your team and focus their energy in a particular creative direction. In either case—briefing or presenting—the purpose of a mood board is to be shown early. The items of a mood board, while illustrative, should be very easy to change if the client hates it.

Style Tiles

After presenting and gaining approval on a mood board, the client might require a greater level of detail before moving forward with the design. For this Web designers create what is known as style tiles. Style tiles provide a higher level of detail to the visual story, but still fall short of an actual layout of a Web page.

As the name implies, style tiles go beyond simply showing an array of elements; they depict specific styles that might be applied to the design elements. For example, a style tile might show a stroke or shadowing effect around photography, how dimension might be used, or how specific type treatments like headlines or body copy might appear.

Information architecture, mood boards, and style tiles are all means of building the experience that is right for a particular target user, and they help designers avoid falling into the cookie-cutter generic design style that is seen all over the Web. The colors, photos, textures, type, etc., that have been established with the mood boards and style tiles are the foundation for the user's experience.

> "The way we think, what we experience, and what we do every day is very much a matter of metaphor."
>
> From the book Metaphors We Live By
> By George Lakoff and Mark Johnson

Metaphors

What mood boards and style tiles help to do is establish a metaphor for a site. A metaphor is defined as "a thing regarded as representative of something else." When designing and interacting with Web pages, it's easy to forget that there aren't actually "buttons" or "tabs" that users "press." Those are just metaphors from the real world of dashboards, calculators, file folders, etc., that have developed into a visual explanation of a clickable item.

Metaphors make the unfamiliar familiar. They take abstract ideas, like linking text from one page to another, and make them tangible. They help users relate to the content and the design of a site. The right metaphor can help reduce the need for instructional copy by creating a setting or environment that is familiar to the audience.

Ultimately, finding the right experience for your user is what designers strive to do. Creating mood boards, style tiles, and developing a visual metaphor are ways in which designers create sites that unique to their clients' brands and right for the desired experience of the target user audience.

The next chapter explores turning these metaphors into meaningful experiences for your target user.

This Web site example from the Museum of Modern Art has no "buttons." It uses a walking metaphor to get users from one point of content to another.

(Opposite) This famous painting by Magritte (c.1929) can remind us that when we're surfing on the Web there are no buttons to be pushed. Only pixels on a screen.

CHAPTER 2

ELEMENTS OF USABILITY

To effectively plan out a Web site project, a designer must have a good understanding of usability. Usability is a term that refers to the ease with which users can learn, engage with, and get satisfaction from an interface for a Web site or piece of software. While the IA documentation, like usability diagrams, is helpful for a designer in planning out a Web site, usability effectiveness also comes from a variety of other factors—design, server speed, technology usage, animation, and even sound effects. This chapter explores the following interface elements, which, when combined, cover the usability touchpoints for a user: navigation, breadcrumbs, site search, submission forms, links and buttons, and error messages. While usability comes from more than just these interface elements, these are the features of a site that a designer can most greatly influence.

Enough About You

Usability is about the user (period). Usability is directly related to the experience a user has with a site—the better the usability, the better the experience is likely to be. Individual users vary widely, even within a single target market. In Web design, standard demographic data such as age, education, gender, language, interests, and culture apply exactly as they do in other forms of communication—but there's an added level of demographic information that includes technology, like operating system, processor speed, screen resolution, memory, and network connection speed. All of this demographic information can play an influential role when it comes to usability design.

Usability is such a critical aspect of Web design that many Web design agencies employ user experience (UX) experts. Part sociologist, part technician, this person is responsible for determining the most appropriate usability based on the abilities and expectations of the target user group, as well as the technology that's available. Some of the factors that usability experts consider include:

Page load times: For desktop, this is less of an issue, since most computers are connected to the Internet with high-speed connections. But for mobile, this is essential. Not only will pages load more quickly, but the site will use less of the user's mobile data allowance.

Legibility: In all cases, the legibility of the typography—including adequate contrast between the type color and the background, sizing, line spacing, and font choice—is essential for increasing the usability of a site. More about this topic in chapter 6.

Handicap Accessibility: While this is mainly a coding practice, it's important for designers to be mindful of things like ALT tags, which are a text description of images. This is particularly important when using images for headlines or buttons. The ALT text is read out loud by browsers with their accessibility setting turned on.

Scannable Content: Users come to a site for content, plain and simple. So the content is a key part of the usability of a site. Content should be broken up into manageable bits with descriptive headings, making pages easily scannable by the user.

Clear URLs and Page Titles: The page title appears in the header of a Web browser and it tells the user what the content of the page is. It also tells search engines what the content of the page is. Accurate and clear page titles help users find the right content.

Consistent Design Treatments: The design of a site needs to hold together and be consistent for the user to be able to recognize various elements of a page. This is also true about the mobile experience of a site. It should share consistent design treatments with the desktop and vice versa.

Cross-channel usability: More than ever, users start browsing for content on mobile and tablet devices. Therefore, UX and Web designers must consider the mobile experience as a critical part of the overall experience of a Web site. The principles of usability that follow are universal, however, the specific design treatments may vary on mobile to increase usability. Wherever possible, examples of desktop and mobile samples are shown.

Navigation

Navigation is a broad term that encompasses any aspect of a site that links a user to another area of the site and is the cornerstone of a site's usability. Unlike other forms of information design that have a natural sequence—pages of a book or brochure, for example—Web pages present users with a menu of options and allow them to choose their own order. The main navigation of a site is the primary set of links that a user clicks to get to the important content of a site. The most common convention for main navigation is a persistent bar across the upper part of a page that features a list of five to seven options, with other options relegated to sub-navigation. (Groups of five to seven are generally what people are capable of perceiving before attempting to break them down into subgroups.)

There are two ways of dealing with large site architectures: Categorize content into main sections, then use a cascading system of menus either with drop-down lists or sub-menus; or break up the list of choices into the most important items (primary navigation) and the lesser important items (secondary navigation). In either case, six groups of five are much easier to comprehend than one group of thirty. Either method makes comprehending the site architecture easier for the user and reduces the number of clicks it takes for a user to get from one place on the site to another.

These images show the drop-down menu navigation on newyorkmag.com. Information is grouped into six main categories for greater usability.

This elaborate drop-down menu on Porsche.com expands to make finding content very easy for the user.

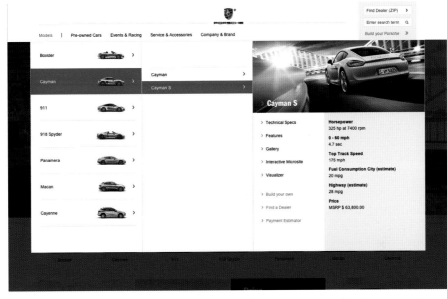

Uncommon and unexpected, the navigation on livwrk.com is at the bottom of the page. The navigation persistently "sticks" to the bottom and over the content.

Navigational elements need to visually stand apart from the rest of the elements on the page and indicate that the user can click on them. There are usually four states to an item in a navigation bar: the dormant or static state; the active state, which indicates the current page; a rollover state, which is sometimes the same as the active state when a user mouses over the button; and the visited state, which indicates to the user what's already been visited. This system should be easy for the user to learn and should remain consistent throughout the entire site.

Navigation can be horizontal or vertical as in this case on the GoogleVentures Web site. The icons help the navigation stand apart from the content and telegraph the content behind the links.

The language of a button should clearly and accurately predict the content of the destination page. The labels should be written from the user's perspective, with terms users might use to find what they're looking for. (Users are quick to abandon a site if they have been confused or deceived by a misleading button.) In addition, since search engines often value the text within links, it's important to use keyword-rich terms in the navigation. This is also why the most effective navigation bars use Web fonts for the buttons—not images of text, which are unreadable by search engines.

The topic of Navigation is explored further from a design perspective in chapter 4, "Anatomy of a Web Page."

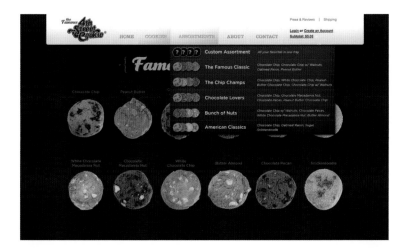

The drop-down menu on FamousCookies.com has not only descriptive copy but small imagery of cookies, making finding the right section easier.

Breadcrumbs

A useful subset of navigation is something called breadcrumb links or breadcrumbs. They are not quite navigation, but they're more prominent than standard text links. Breadcrumb links reveal to the user the path taken through the site architecture to get to the current page, thus making it easier to go back. The name breadcrumbs comes from the story of Hansel and Gretel, when Hansel scattered crumbs of bread on the ground to help him and his sister find their way home. Unfortunately for the pair, birds came along and ate their breadcrumbs, but the metaphor lives on as a trail of tasty links guiding users on Web sites.

A form of breadcrumbing is also used for submission forms. An indicator bar is sometimes used across the top of a form to reveal the number of steps in the process—both what they've completed as well as the steps yet to come. This helps estimate how long a submission form is and whether it's worth the user's time to complete.

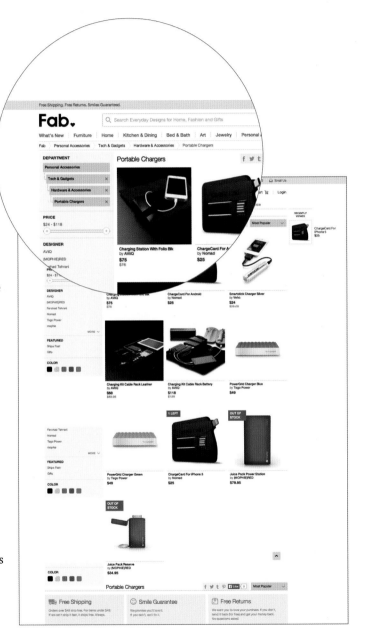

Breadcrumb links like those seen in these samples act as a sub-navigation that lights a user's way back to the home page.

Breadcrumbs can be simple links or more elaborate drop-down menus like the ones seen above. In both cases they help the user ground himself or herself on the site.

The limited color palette of Joyent.com helps the orange text links stand apart from the other content on the page while still maintaining an overall color harmony on the page.

Links and Buttons

Within the content of a site, it's often necessary to link users to other areas of the site for additional content. This granular level of navigation is helpful to users who want to know more about a specific idea, and helpful for SEO because linked words have high indexing value. Since linked text usually consists of keywords from the article, highlighting the links helps the "scannability" of a page—a user can scan and read the linked words and get a general sense for the content of the page. Links in long bodies of text, however, can also be a distraction to a user who's trying to focus on a single story. For this reason, links should stand out so they can be recognized, but not so much so that they're distracting.

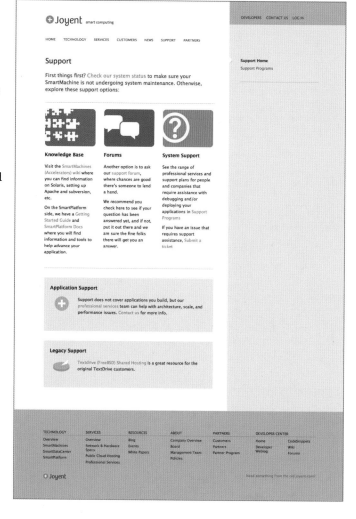

These examples from AndyRutledge.com (top) and JustWatchTheSky.com (below) show alternate ways to highlight links. Any CSS style variation is possible when indicating links, from underlining and color changes to size, weight, and background color shifts.

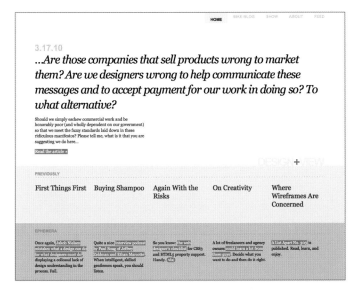

According to leading usability authority Jakob Nielsen (useit.com), the best method for indicating a text link is underlining and changing the color of linked text; however, any alteration is available when indicating a link in CSS. Aside from the indication of a link, there should also be two other visual states of a link: mouse over, and visited. The mouse-over state gives the user visual feedback that the text is indeed a link and not just underlined for emphasis. The visited state helps the user recognize where he or she has been. There's also a less common active state, which appears the moment a user clicks.

Site Search

Perhaps the quickest way to allow users to find information on a Web site is through a site search feature. Search forms search a database of site content and display the results for a user, linking them directly to the item they came for—ideally. Because a search box is intended to increase usability, it should be as easy to find and use as possible. This means placing it above the fold in a conspicuous location that's consistent on every page and clearly labeled "Search" or something similar. Also, it's important to make the search field long enough to accommodate the types of searches people will conduct. Although longer search terms can be entered into a short field, users tend to edit themselves if they're given a small space. It is also possible to pre-populate the search form with the type of search available through the form.

Internal site searches will sometimes have an advanced search feature. This is an extension of the search functionality with added fields that allow a user to narrow down a search to increase the likelihood of finding what is needed. The most effective search boxes have the ability to remember popular searches and match them to the characters entered by the user so the user can see, then click on, a list of potential search terms and be redirected to those results.

The search features on Typography.com, which includes "find fonts" and "browse collections" drop-down features, make finding content on the site easy and intuitive.

Usability Testing

While creative focus groups can be the death of fresh ideas, usability testing, which consists of inviting potential users to complete a series of tasks using the interface concept, can greatly help refine the usability elements of a site. During a usability test session, the moderator observes and records the users' reactions and emotions as they attempt to complete a given task. Confusion or frustration expressed by the user help pinpoint trouble spots, whereas delight or satisfaction means that the usability is appropriate for the task and the user.

To the right is a sample transcript from a usability test. In this example the subject tester is asked to find books about graphic design. The moderator prompts the user with tasks and nothing more. The user's actions and quotes are recorded and the icons indicate positive or negative feedback, as well as feedback that represents an idea by the user.

First impressions

"I like the design and the colors, but I don't know where to begin. I suppose if I had something to do here I would know where to start."

Please search for information about graphic design books.
Subject starts search

"The search field is a bit short, which makes me think I can only search for single terms."

Subject receives 18 results.

"It would be great if these results could be sorted by price and availability."

Subject really likes the layout of the results page, including the thumbnail images of the books.

Please select a book for purchase
Subject clicks the thumbnail of the book to view detail and nothing happens.

"I should be able to click the image of the book to see the product descriptions."

Subject clicks "Learn More" and sees product description page.

"I like this page, but it's too hard to find the price. I want to know immediately how much this book costs."

Subject adds book to shopping cart.

"I like how I don't leave the page when the book is added to the cart."

Subject clicks the "Check Out" link and proceeds to check out page.

The search field is only half of a site search solution; the **search results page** is the other.

The search field is only half of a site search solution; the search results page is the other. There are a couple of important features of a results page that can help with usability. The searched term should remain in the search box at the top of the page and the number of results found should also clearly be displayed. Effective search results pages give users the ability to sort the results—by date, by relevance, or by author, for example. The search results themselves should display enough key information so the user can make an informed decision as to whether the results are the desired ones. Finally, on the article page, there should be a mechanism that allows users to rate the relevance and quality of the article based on the user's search criteria. This will teach the search engines what content is most relevant for different search terms.

The search results on Gap.com feature photos of the clothing related to the search by the user. The search results also have a filtering feature which makes narrowing down the selections easy.

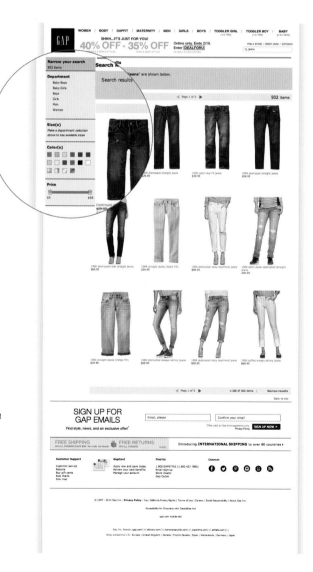

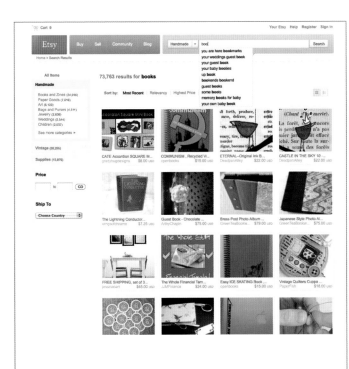

Etsy.com has a very clean top navigation with an equally intuitive search feature. The search area starts with a drop-down menu of categories, followed by a search field that offers popular search suggestions based on the letters a user types in. The search results (bottom) are sortable and can be converted from image view to list view.

GoWalla.com displays search results in two ways; on a map and in a list. This gives the user more options for finding the content they are looking for.

As a general rule, users don't like filling out forms, so it's the job of the designer and UX specialist to make the process as **pain-free** as possible.

Submission Forms

Submission forms, where a user inputs information and submits it to the site, generally represent a goal for a site—inviting the user to register, sign up for a newsletter, buy a product—so the usability of a submission form is of premium importance. Unfortunately, as a general rule, users don't like filling out forms, so it's the job of the designer and UX specialist to make the process as pain-free as possible. It's important to be clear about the length of the form up front, with long forms broken up into manageable segments with a breadcrumb trail indicating what's left to come.

A form is a series of fields that a user fills out with information. The fields should be clearly labeled with the information that needs to go in them. Designing the labels to the left of the field, as opposed to above them, will give the appearance of a shorter form. Required and optional fields should be indicated clearly so the user knows what fields can be skipped. Fields should be grouped in a logical way so the user can follow the flow easily, and redundant information, such as shipping versus billing information, should be pre-populated if the user desires. When validation (an available username, for example) is required, it should be given in process, not after the form has been submitted. The number of times a user has to correct errors and resubmit a form greatly increases the likelihood that the user will drop off.

CONTACT

Adding style to a submission form can make it more inviting for the user. The forms seen here, from the simple email form above to the more complex content management forms on the opposite page, benefit from a clear grid, generous white space, and typographic hierarchy.

These form examples from Threadless.com (top) and CollabFinder.com (bottom) utilize an underlying grid structure to organize the space in the layout, which helps minimize the appearance of large amounts of information to fill in.

It's often useful for a designer to limit the number of actions a user can take when on a form page. This can mean removing all global navigation and limiting the clickable options to "Submit" and possibly some "Help" links. After submitting a form, a user should be given a clear indication that the submission was successful.

Get Started with a Free Account

Sign up in 30 seconds. No credit card required. If you
already have a MailChimp account log in.

Email

What's your email address?

Username

Password

☐ Show

Create My Account

By clicking this button, you agree to MailChimp's Anti-spam Policy
& Terms of Use.

MailChimp

©2001–2014 All Rights Reserved. MailChimp® is a registered
trademark of The Rocket Science Group. Privacy and Terms

*These form examples from MailChimp.com (top)
and OmmWriter.com (bottom) style the form
elements in a way that causes them to blend in
with the design. Although rarely taken advantage
of, CSS can style form fields just like any other
element within a design.*

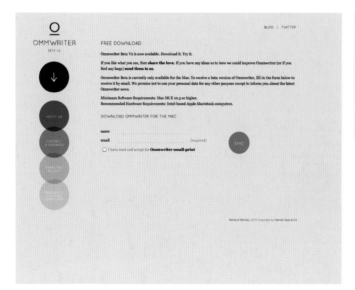

Each **form element** has a specific purpose that a designer should understand when designing an online form.

Form Title

Input 1

Password

Input 2

◉ Option 1
Single-line description copy for option 1

○ Option 2
Single-line description copy for option 2

○ Option 3
Single-line description copy for option 3

Selection 1

| Select ▼ |

Selection 2

☒ Choice 1

☐ Choice 2

Action

This sample form shows the various form elements that are used to collect information. Each element has a specific purpose that a designer should understand when designing an online form.

There are three types of text fields: text box collects a single line of information; text box with password protection collects a single line of information but the user only sees bullets or asterisks; and text area, which can collect multiple lines of text. Text fields can be set to be pre-populated with a phrase to help the user understand the type of information that can be input.

For selecting items there are three main choices: radio buttons (seen as circles in this diagram) are mutually exclusive—meaning only one can be selected from a group—and they allow for written explanations of the options; drop-down menus are also mutually exclusive and they provide a simple list of items; and check boxes (seen as boxes in this diagram), which are used for allowing the user to select multiple options.

The submit button triggers the action of a form and can either be a browser-generated user interface (UI) element, an image, or text.

Error Messages

Despite the best efforts of designers and UX experts, users will sometimes come across an error on a site. The most common errors on submission forms occur when the proper information is not filled in correctly. Indicating an error clearly can be essential in converting users who are willing to spend time filling out a form. To clearly indicate an error, a designer should visually separate the error message from the page so the user easily notices it. The content of the message should be clear yet polite, and the offending form should be highlighted clearly so the user can find it quickly and make the correction.

This example from OnSugar.com is not an error, but a hint that appears as the user selects the various form fields. This proactive approach can help reduce the need for error messaging altogether.

The sign-up form on Dunked.com starts off with an X on the username field and turns to a check when a usable name is typed in the field.

In the lower example on this page—barleysgville.com—the error message is displayed as a single line below the form, with a list of the missed fields.

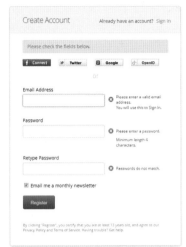

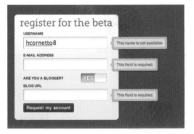

These examples range from subtle markings to obvious red fields and caution icons. The right level of strength for the error message depends as much on the layout environment it appears in as the experience level of the user group that will be using the site.

"Something went technically wrong.
Thanks for noticing—we're going to fix it
up and have things back to normal soon."

The right copy can play an important role in
effective error messaging, since it's easy for the
user to feel like he or she has done something
wrong. In this example from Twitter.com, the
copy reads, "Something went technically wrong.
Thanks for noticing—we're going to fix it up and
have things back to normal soon."

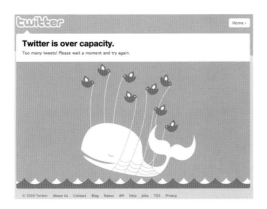

The "Fail Whale," also from Twitter.com, is a
surprising yet delightful error message. The
unexpected nature of a whale being flown by birds
makes finding an error almost forgivable.

The surprising number of hits a 404 page receives makes it a **prime design opportunity** to direct the user and reinforce the client's brand.

Another form of error message is the "404 Page Not Found." Often overlooked by designers, this page appears when a user lands on a URL that no longer exists or never existed. The surprising number of hits a 404 page gets makes it a prime design opportunity to direct the user and reinforce the client's brand. Custom 404 pages should be somewhat apologetic in tone and present a series of links so the user can find what he or she originally was looking for. The ability to search or even report the missing page is an additional feature that can be added to a 404 page.

This custom 404 page from Heinz.com combines both an element of humor and the utility of being able to find information on the site.

Surprise and Delight

While the Web has many utilitarian aspects to it, it's also important to remember that users—people—enjoy being entertained. "Surprise and delight" is a phrase adopted from the hospitality industry and used by Web designers and UX specialists to describe the fun or unexpected features of a site. (This should not be confused with "mislead and confuse.") Surprise and delight refers to added value for a user—something that goes beyond expectations. Surprise and delight can be humorous, irreverent, or even seductive. Exactly what kind of surprise is appropriate, like anything else, depends on the target audience.

The 404 pages seen here and on the next spread are prime examples of surprise and delight.

These custom 404 pages from huwshimi.com (top) and teez.com.au (center and bottom) illustrate a sense of the company's brands, both with a sense of beauty and humor.

We looked everywhere.

And couldn't find that page. But we did find these under the couch cushions.

Not what you're looking for? Try the links below:

Personal Finance Solution
Mint.com

Personal Finance Mobile Apps
Overview | iPhone | iPad | Android

Personal Finance Blog
MintLife.com

Nothing to see here
We can't find /404/

Please use the navigation above or search to find what you're looking for.

Search MailChimp

MailChimp

©2001–2014 All Rights Reserved. MailChimp® is a registered trademark of The Rocket Science Group.

The custom 404 pages on this page from Mint.com (top), MailChimp.com (center), and DisneyStore.com (bottom) have a sense of brand but also provide a means for the user to find the content he or she was seeking—from a site nav and links to a search field.

CHAPTER 3

SPACE, GRIDS & RESPONSIVE DESIGN

In the final step of the planning phase of a Web design project, the designer begins to prepare the canvas for a design. This means developing a grid system that is flexible enough to accommodate a variety of content, but rigid enough to form a recognizable system. Grids are fundamentally about space, and this chapter explores means of organizing space to enhance a user's access to, and understanding of, information.

Organization & Hierarchy

One of the most important aspects of design is the concept of hierarchy. Visual hierarchy is the sequencing of elements within a design so that a user may perceive them in a specific and logical order. This sequence clearly defines the most important elements of the design, followed by the second most important elements, and so on. Almost every type of information can be broken down into three or four levels of importance. More than that makes contrasting the difference between the levels difficult.

An effective **design system** takes precedence over the individual elements, so that the user perceives a cohesive unit.

To create hierarchy, a designer must first create a system. A system is created by logically grouping the elements of a design, either through meaning or function, and forming visual relationships between them. An effective design system takes precedence over the individual elements so that the user perceives a cohesive unit. Any element that breaks this system will have more visual value and be understood to have more importance than the other elements, creating a hierarchy.

For example, in a classroom where the desks are neatly arranged in five rows of five desks and each student is sitting in his or her seat, the students appear as a single unit. Regardless of the different genders, clothing, hair styles, or body types, all the students fit within the group because of their organization or spatial relationship to one another. If a single student decided to break the system of rows by moving his desk into the aisle, he would stand apart from the system and give himself visual importance over the other students. The students appear as a single unit because of their arrangement in space—the rows of desks—and the student whose desk is not in line with the others stands out strictly because of his lack of relationship, or his contrast, with the others.

White Space

Creating a design system almost always starts with the clear organization of space. Deliberately constructed white space, not to be confused with unconsidered or empty space, is often overlooked as an element of Web design. In fact, a common mistake among inexperienced designers is to focus too heavily on the "objects" in a design (type, images, points, lines, and planes), and space is simply what's left over when they're finished. Space is essential for creating relationships that form systems that lead to a clear hierarchy of elements. It should not be underestimated.

The interplay between the objects of a design and the background is called the figure-ground relationship. White space, also called negative space, is a reference to the "ground" in "figure-ground." The goal of a designer is to achieve a balance between figure and ground, where one doesn't completely dominate the other. Instead, they work together to unify the design.

White space design elements include: **margins,** the area surrounding a design; **gutters,** the space between columns of a grid; **padding,** the area around an element contained by a border; **line spacing,** also known as leading, the space from baseline to cap height between lines of text; and **paragraph spacing,** the space between paragraphs or separate ideas in a piece of text. Adding line space is the most common form of paragraph indication in Web design, although it is possible to use other methods like indenting, which is also another form of white space utilization.

These elements are arranged with no consideration of the space within the layout.

The same elements as above are now grouped and the space has been more clearly defined and organized.

The organization of the space in the layout creates a natural hierarchy or sequence of importance by either relating or separating elements.

The Gestalt Principles of Perception:
"The whole is greater than the sum of the parts."

Theories involving the psychology of visual organization within art and design come mostly from the Gestalt Principles of Perception. These principles, developed in the early twentieth century at the Staatliches Bauhaus in Germany, refer to the mind's ability to group elements based on one of the following relationships:

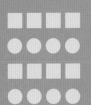 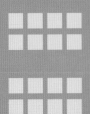 

SIMILARITY
Grouping of elements that have a unique visual relationship. The two rows of squares above are grouped, despite being separated by a row of circles. The relationship of shape takes precedence over the spacial relationships.

PROXIMITY
Grouping of elements that are close to one another. Two groups are perceived above, despite the fact that there are sixteen individual boxes.

CLOSURE
Grouping of elements that complete a larger unit. A single square is perceived in the above illustration, despite several of the smaller units being removed. The small square in the upper right "closes" the spacing to create a single form.

CONTINUANCE
Grouping of elements that complete a pattern or progression. Each row of boxes above forms a group despite the gaps in the row.

Deliberately constructed white space,
not to be confused with leftover, unconsidered, or empty space, is often overlooked as a useful element of Web design.

InformationArchitects.jp (opposite) uses a minimalist design that relies heavily on the use of white space to organize information and create hierarchy. The gutters, line spacing, and paragraph spacing are carefully crafted to help the user identify individual groups of information.

Similarly, JonTangerine.com (this page) uses wide margins and ample padding to make the page design scannable. With the exception of a small dot of yellow and a bit of red at the bottom, this black-and-white layout uses only a single font (Georgia) yet it has a clear hierarchy of information and plenty of visual interest.

Elements of a Web design aren't just design elements, they're the **interface** that the user needs to navigate and find information

The use of hierarchy and white space in Web design has a bit of extra significance over their use in other forms of communication, since the elements of a design aren't just elements, they're the interface that the user needs to navigate and find information. The primary navigation bar, for example, needs to be immediately identifiable as such, so that the user can navigate the site. The design conventions discussed in the previous chapter help the user identify specific areas of a Web site, but they shouldn't be taken for granted. Guiding the user through a layout should be done deliberately to ensure maximum usability.

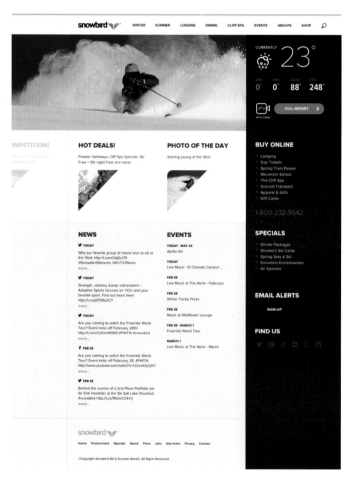

The example shown here from SnowBird.com uses white space around the imagery to mimic the branding and give the page an "ownable" feature.

PRODUCTS   STORY   PARTNERS   IMPACT   mettā
                                                 SKINCARE   JOURNAL   STOCKISTS   CONTACT   BUY ONLINE

Mettā Skincare is a range of natural
skincare products created for you and your
skin with an environmental and
social consciousness.

Learn more about Metta Skincare ⌄

ABOUT

Mettā Skincare is a range of natural skincare products created for you and
your skin with an environmental and social consciousness. Using 100%
natural ingredients and established relationships with local and international
artisan producers, Mettā Skincare is more than just a product range. It is a
conscious lifestyle choice that will leave you feeling good about your skin
and the earth.

STORY

PARTNERS

IMPACT

LATEST JOURNAL POSTS

JANUARY 17 – 2014
Looking After Your Skin In Summer

NOVEMBER 28 – 2013
Why Natural Skincare

NOVEMBER 19 – 2013
Guide to Naturally Beautiful Skin

NOVEMBER 19 – 2013
Getting the most out of Mettā Skincare
products

This sample, MettaSkinCare.com, uses generous white space to give the page, and the product, a premium feel. Nothing is cluttered; every design element is given "air."

White space is also essential for making a layout scannable, a critical aspect of Web design. Layouts with well-managed white space allow users to scan information and groups of information to find what they're looking for quickly. Cluttered layouts, or ones that don't effectively manage white space, make it hard for the user to identify patterns which are essential for scanning information. Imagine a group of people milling around at a party versus a line of soldiers at roll call. The people are the same, but the space between them has been organized.

This is a side-by-side comparison of a competition mini-site created by the AIGA DC. On the left is the original site; on the right the white space has been filled in to highlight the consistent and almost rhythmical use of space. The generous spacing around the headline and lead-in statement helps them stand out on the page. The non-default, slightly open line spacing for all the text gives the pages a very light and scannable feel.

White space is actually a reference to "ground" as in "figure-ground," and doesn't need to be white at all. In this example, ThinkingForALiving.com, the ground is a pink hue, but the result of well-constructed white space on the design is the same.

Containment

At times, more than space is needed to highlight, group, or separate elements on a page. Borders, lines, and boxes can be helpful in defining the space and containing elements within sub-groups. The varying types of borders that can be created with CSS, including dotted, dashed, double, and single lines, make them powerful stylistic elements as well. Even rounded corners, a popular design treatment for boxes, are now possible using CSS3, and they are viewable in browsers compatible with CSS3.

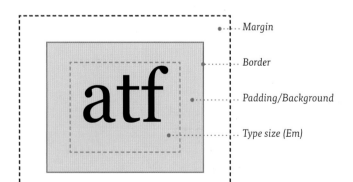

Margin

Border

Padding/Background

Type size (Em)

The sites seen here, BrandNew.UnderConsideration.com (top), and 20x200.com (bottom) use a wide variety of distinctive line styles to segment the page and reinforce a design style.

(Left) CSS can be used to define the border of an object. The border, represented by the orange line in this diagram, lies between the padding distance and the margin area.

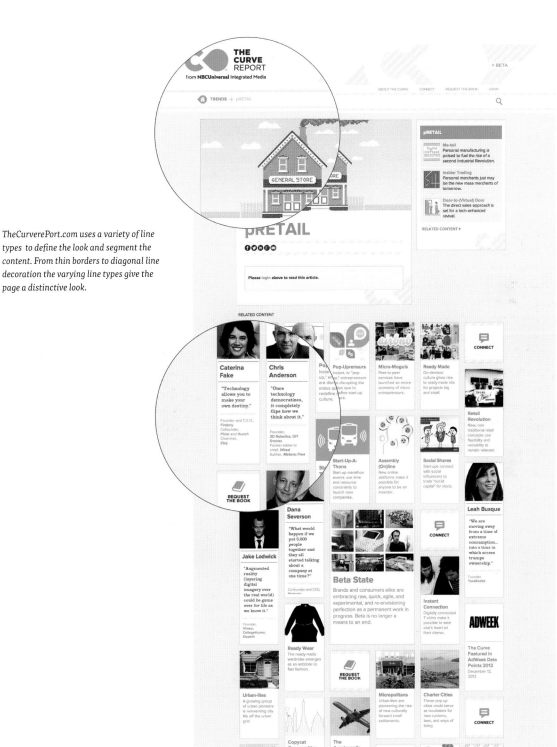

TheCurverePort.com uses a variety of line types to define the look and segment the content. From thin borders to diagonal line decoration the varying line types give the page a distinctive look.

Grids not only organize the elements of a design, they organize the **space** within a design.

Grids

One of the oldest ways to create a balance of figure and ground is through the use of a grid system. Grids not only organize the elements of a design, they organize the space within a design. Clearly aligning design elements through the use of columns creates defined space, and it's this space that gives the appearance of organization.

Grids are made up of columns (where the content goes), gutters (the space between columns and margins), and the space around the perimeter of the layout. By carefully defining these attributes, Web designers can control the density of a page, which is the amount of detail that is visible to the user. Dense pages tend to be harder to read, although pages that lack sufficient density can appear un-unified and fall apart.

Early Web sites were laid out using tables, a word processing convention of rows and columns used to arrange elements. Some early Web layouts had a compartmentalized or checkerboard feel as a result of using or overusing tables. Tables are also limited in their flexibility and result in long markup for even simple layouts. Although tables still exist in HTML, <div> or divider tags have taken over as the preferred method of containing and laying out elements of a design. The flexibility of CSS-styled <div> tags more closely resembles the feel of a print layout program such as Adobe InDesign. They enable very sophisticated, print-like layout and grid use.

New Graphic Design magazine was started in 1958 by Richard Paul Lahose, Josef Müller-Bockmann, Hans Neuburg, and Carlo Vivarelle. The cover of issue 16, pictured here, illustrates the grid system that permeated the entire magazine and is credited with defining the Swiss style of graphic design.

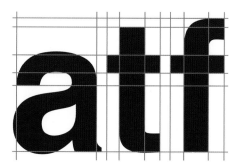

The letterforms of Helvetica, the ubiquitous Swiss typeface and subject of a documentary film, are based on a grid system, making it instantly recognizable over its predecessor, Akzidenz Grotesque.

Neue Grafik
New Graphic Design
Graphisme actuel

Internationale Zeitschrift für Grafik und verwandte Gebiete
Text dreisprachig (deutsch, englisch, französisch)

International Review of Graphic Design and related subjects
Issued in German, English and French

Revue internationale du graphisme et des domaines annexes
Parution en langue allemande, anglaise et française

16

Ausgabe Juli 1963

Issue for July 1963

Juillet 1963

Inhalt

Contents

Table des matières

Einzelnummer Fr. 15.–

Single number Fr. 15.–

Le numéro Fr. 15.–

Herausgeber und Redaktion
Editors and Managing Editors
Editeurs et rédaction

Druck Verlag
Printing/Publishing
Imprimerie Edition

Richard P. Lohse SWB/VSG, Zürich
J. Müller-Brockmann SWB/VSG, Zürich
Hans Neuburg SWB/VSG, Zürich
Carlo L. Vivarelli SWB/VSG, Zürich

Walter-Verlag AG, Olten
Schweiz Switzerland/Suisse

Pattern Library
Grid System

Grid System

Typography

Form Elements

Navigation

Tables

Lists

Stats

Stats/Data

Feedback

The design team at MailChimp.com gives users a glimpse at their design system with their Pattern Library. This tool reveals the systems, including this grid system behind the site.

Grid sizes Grid gutter Mixed grids Responsive columns Grid example

Our grid system is composed of 8 flexible columns with a gutter between columns of 30px. We apply border-box so that the border and padding is included in the width of the grid columns.

Grid Sizes

Size 1 of 1

Size 1 of 2

Size 1of 3

Size 1of 4

Size 1of 8

```
1  <div class="line">
2    <div class="unit size1of3">
3    </div>
4    <div class="unit size1of">
5    </div>
6    <div class="lastUnit size1of3">
7    </div>
8  </div>
9
```

Notes

When using the grid, wrap the columns using a line and use lastUnit for the last column. Refer to OOCSS base classes to learn more about the grid classes.

This example applies to the other ratios we support: 1/1, 1/2, 1/3, 1/4, and 1/8

Grid gutter

Our grid columns have a 15px padding on either side that results in a 30px gutter between columns and a 15px gutter on the grid edges. Even though our columns are fluid, the gutter remains constant.

Mixed Grids

The grid layout is easily extended by nesting and mixing different column sizes.

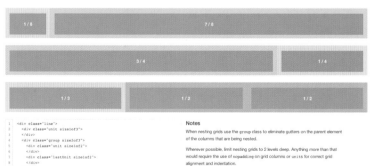

```
1   <div class="line">
2     <div class="unit size1of3">
3     </div>
4     <div class="group size2of3">
5       <div class="unit size1of2">
6       </div>
7       <div class="lastUnit size1of2">
8       </div>
9     </div>
10  </div>
11
```

Notes

When nesting grids use the group class to eliminate gutters on the parent element of the columns that are being nested.

Wherever possible, limit nesting grids to 2 levels deep. Anything more than that would require the use of nopadding on grid columns or units for correct grid alignment and indentation.

CRW / CORPORATE RISK WATCH

Profile
who we are

Services
what we can do

Case Studies
problem solutions

Regions
where we operate

Contact
enquire here

Due Diligence

An international oil company was considering entering into a business relationship with an oil and gas producer in the Philippines but suspected that the target company was associated with local politically exposed persons and that this association might have favoured the company in obtaining a concession for oil extraction. To comply with the Foreign Corruption Practices Act regulations it was necessary to conduct an extensive due diligence to assess the potential risks attached to the deal.

A systematic analysis of publicly available documentation in the Philippines and discreet source enquiries into the target company and its principals were conducted.

It emerged that the management of the oil producer in the Philippines was composed of highly experienced and prominent figures from the public energy sector who continued to retain significant political influence. The beneficial owner of the company in the Philippines was hiding behind nominees and offshore structures but his identity was revealed through discreet source enquiries in the local energy sector. It emerged that the ultimate beneficial owner was a former representative of the local government and that his political influence enabled the company to obtain the said concession. The risks attached to the target company were assessed.

Competitor Intelligence

A British company operating in the IT sector was interested in the purchase of one of its three Italian competitors but was unable to put in place the right strategy without having an in-depth knowledge of the Italian IT sector and specifically, the three target companies. In addition the client suspected that one of the players had links to the Organised Crime but was unable to assess the veracity of this rumour.

The work conducted included analysis of the financial situation, business models, investments, marketing and product strategies with respect to each of the three companies through a systematic retrieval, analysis and cross examination of publicly available information, combined with discreet source enquiries with local industry experts.

The work resulted in the identification of one of the tree competitors as the potential acquisition target. Evidence was obtained confirming the allegation of association with organised crime by one of the target companies.

Litigation Support

A Dutch operator in the printing sector suspected that a former employer, an engineer who had worked for the company for over twenty years and who had recently retired, was providing a competitor with the company's know how and other confidential data such as supplier and client contacts. To get these activities to stop, the Dutch operator initiated a legal proceedings against the competitor and its former employees but did not have sufficient evidence to prove the case.

The work conducted consisted in collecting evidence, both factual and testimonial in support to the client's claim, including surveillance and witness identification.

The client was able prove with factual evidence the case of unfair competition. The competitor stopped to act unfairly and the client received compensation for the damages suffered.

CRW / CORPORATE RISK WATCH

Profile
who we are

Services
what we can do

Case Studies
problem solutions

Regions
where we operate

Contact
enquire here

CRW relies on a multi-lingual team with international experience in risk management and on a network of contracted professionals worldwide.

The success of our clients' businesses is influenced by decisions taken with respect to new partnerships, investments and business dealings.

CRW's skilled team of multi-lingual professionals with international experience helps clients mitigate the exposure to financial and reputational risks.

CRW provides clients with reliable information and strategic analysis they require to maximise business opportunities in different regions of the world.

CRW offers services to comply with anti-corruption and anti-money laundering legislations and in support of business partnerships, investments and market entries, hiring of employees, complicated business transactions and legal disputes.

Memberships

Corporate Risk Watch is the holder of a private investigations license, in accordance with the paragraph 134 T.U.L.P.S. issued by the Italian authorities.

Corporate Risk Watch is a member of the following associations:

Association of anti-money Laundering Specialists (www.acams.org); Italian-American Chamber of Commerce in Italy (www.amcham.it); Italian-Chinese Chamber of Commerce in Italy (www.china-italy.it)

Left Loft, the designers of CorporateRiskWatch.com, actually expose the grid structure they're using by tracing it with dotted lines. The elements of every page seem to dance around this five-column grid.

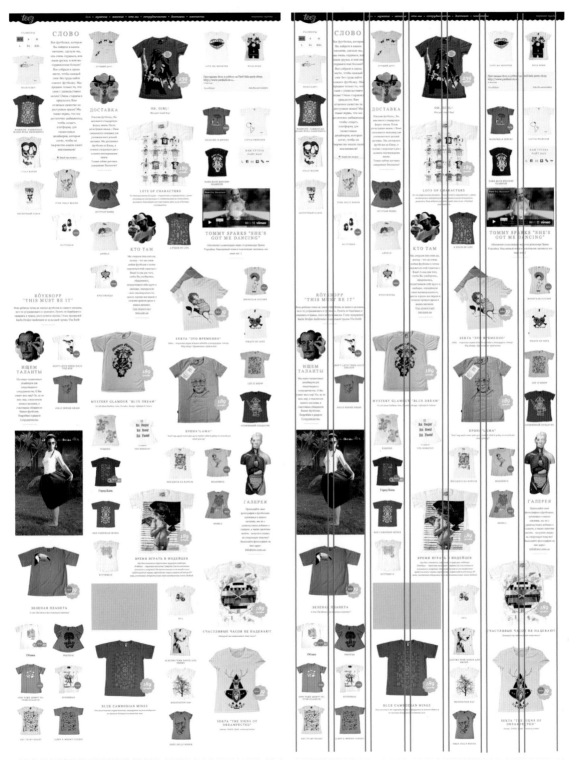

BlackEstate.co.nz, which has won numerous awards for its use of typography and unique navigation, features a six-column grid. The tall page is held together because of the strict adherence to the elegant grid.

The Swiss styling of WilsonMinor.com is a classic example of a well-used grid structure. Headlines, subheads, images, and text work together to define and span the six-column grid.

The grid on DigitalPodge.com is filled in a more organic way. Instead of the elements neatly aligning in exactly the same way, there's a playful bouncing of text and image within the grid structure.

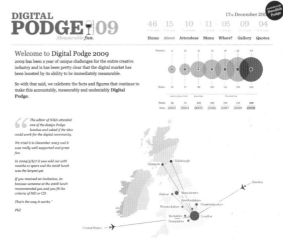

Once the grid system has been established, elements of the design are placed within the grid. Objects can span more than one column width, but each element must have some clear relationship to the grid itself. Any element that relates to the grid in a unique way or breaks the grid system will rank higher on the hierarchy scale.

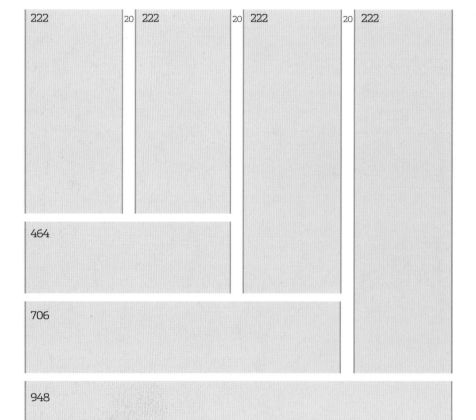

222   20   222   20   222   20   222

464

706

948

This is a diagram of a grid system with the following specifications:
Width: 948px
Columns: 4
Column width: 222px
Gutter width: 20px
2-col span: 464px
3-col span: 706px

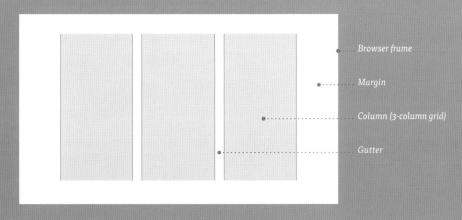

Browser frame

Margin

Column (3-column grid)

Gutter

FIXED WIDTH (Floating Centered; Fixed Left)

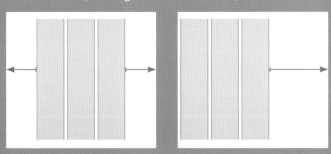

Grids used for Web design need to have a flexible quality to them in order to accommodate varying monitor widths and resolutions. There are several solutions to this issue. In this example of a fixed-width grid, the grid either floats in the center of the browser window or is fixed to the left side. As the browser window expands in both cases, the layout within the grid is not altered.

VARIABLE WIDTH

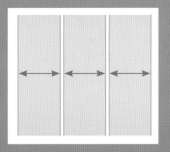

In a variable-width grid system, each column expands proportionately with the width of the browser frame. This causes the layout within the grid to change and shift depending on the width of the user's monitor.

COMBINATION OF VARIABLE AND FIXED
WIDTH

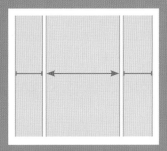

This diagram shows a grid that has both fixed-width columns as well as a single variable-width column. As the browser window expands, only one column width expands with it. The layout of the center column shifts, while the two flanking columns stay fixed.

The grid system on SimpleArt.com.au is flexible, so whether the page is viewed on large or small monitors the layout feels consistent. Note in the wider layout below, the columns of the grid widen and the header/navigation area moves to the right.

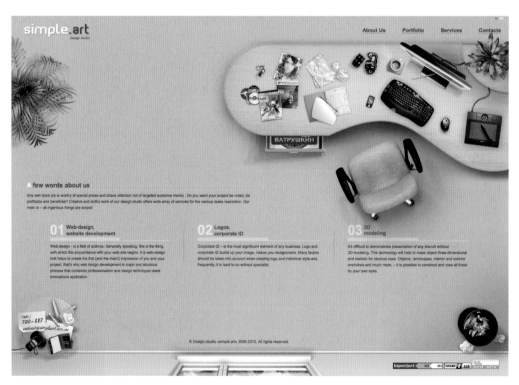

Once the grid system has been established, elements of the design are placed within the grid. Objects can span more than one column width, but each element must have some clear relationship to the grid itself. Any element that relates to the grid in a unique way or breaks the grid system will rank higher on the hierarchy scale.

Items in a layout that break the established system stand apart from the rest of the elements within the system. In this example of AIGALosAngelese.org, the AIGA logo does not "sit" on the grid. By shifting outside the grid it's given more visual value than the other elements on the page, as illustrated in this diagram.

The Baseline Grid

Something that print designers have been using for years but is only recently being adopted by Web designers is the use of a baseline grid. A baseline grid is a horizontal grid system that exactly aligns the baselines of all the text on a page, regardless of size or style. Baseline grids create a smooth rhythm in the typography within a design.

Creating a baseline grid in CSS involves a bit of math, since there's no built-in baseline grid attribute. A Web designer starts by choosing a type size for the majority of the text on the page. Then a line height is applied in the CSS, which is essentially the equivalent of leading. To create the appearance of a baseline grid, all other measurements, including the margin spacing, display type size, etc., should be multiples of the line height. This will ensure that all baselines will line up relative to one another.

TheGridSystem.org is a blog about the use of grids in design. An interesting feature of this site is the ability to expose the grid structure as well as the baseline grid.

Below is an example of a baseline grid in use. Note that each typographic element, regardless of size or typeface, sits exactly on the baseline grid.

Above the Fold

Understanding the Principles of Successful Web Site Design

Jaded zombies acted quietly but kept driving their oxen forward. The wizard quickly jinxed the gnomes before they vaporized. All questions asked by five watched experts amaze the judge. Six boys guzzled cheap raw plum vodka quite joyfully. Just keep examining every low bid quoted for zinc etchings. Sixty zippers were quickly picked from the woven jute bag. Few black taxis drive up major roads on quiet hazy nights. Six big devils from Japan quickly forgot how to waltz. Painful zombies quickly watch a jinxed graveyard. Jaded zombies acted quietly but kept driving their oxen forward. The wizard quickly jinxed the gnomes before they vaporized. All questions asked by five watched experts amaze the judge. Six boys guzzled cheap raw plum vodka quite joyfully. Just keep examining every low bid quoted for zinc etchings. Sixty zippers were quickly picked from the woven jute bag. Few black taxis drive up major roads on quiet hazy nights. Six big devils from Japan quickly forgot how to waltz. Painful zombies quickly watch a jinxed graveyard.

The wizard quickly jinxed the gnomes before they vaporized. All questions asked by five watched experts amaze the judge.

Responsive Design

This chapter is about space. Responsive design is about reorganizing space to maximize the visibility of key design elements on varying screen sizes. Responsive design is an evolution of Web layout because of the prevalence of people browsing Web pages on mobile devices. Design considerations for small screens is vastly different than for large desktop screens, hence the need for a design to respond/change based on the size of the screen on which it is being viewed.

Responsive design is much more than the simple re-arrangement or stacking of content "blocks" so that they run vertically down a slender mobile screen. Great responsive design also takes into account things like page load times and typographic legibility to completely change the content and design of a page for mobile devices. With responsive design a designer can hide large imagery on a mobile device, or change the color and size of type to increase the contrast and legibility.

Without getting too technical, responsive design works through what are called CSS (cascading style sheet) media queries. These media queries read a user's browser data to determine the width of the browser window before loading the styling for a page. Currently, there are three primary break points that designers use for their media queries: larger than 768 pixels wide (desktop), less than 768 pixels (tablet) and less than 480 pixels wide (mobile device).

Left Screenshot (Desktop)

TIME

f y g+ t Apps

Search TIME

Home   NewsFeed   U.S.   Politics   World   Business   Tech   Health   Science   Entertainment   Video   TIME 100   Photos

Magazine   LIFE   Opinion   Weather

Thursday, February 20, 2014

■ Breaking Al-Jazeera journalists trial starts in Egypt

Bulent Kilic / AFP / Getty Images

Allies Abandon Ukraine Leader

By Simon Shuster / Kiev

The nation's embattled President finds his inner circle becoming increasingly smaller as the revolution's death toll climbs

- E.U. Imposes Sanctions on Ukrainian Officials
- Battleground Kiev: 'Halfway Between a War and A Protest'
- Ukraine Inches Ever Closer to a Full-Blown Civil War
- Ukrainian Skier Withdraws From Olympics to Protest at Home

2 Americans Found Dead on *Captain Phillips* Ship

Pussy Riot Releases Music Video of Sochi Beating

VIDEO

Kiev's Frontline From Instagram: A View From The Ground

00:90   01:41

Embed   Email   Share

Kiev's Frontline From Instagram: A View From The Ground

'The Lego Movie' Animators Show How the Film Was Made

Korean Families Reunite After 60 Years of Separation

POLITICS

Hollywood Is Coming to Capitol Hill

Obama and Canadian Leader Make Beer Bet on Olympic Women's Hockey Final

George Bush Misses Air Force One

WORLD

E.U. Imposes Sanctions on Ukrainian Officials

Al-Jazeera Journalists Trial Starts in Egypt

Pussy Riot's New Music Video Shows Sochi Beatdown

BUSINESS

Samsung's Ruthless New Ad Mocks Apple's Latest

Target Shoppers Shrug Off Massive Credit Card Data Breach

The Surprising Best Thing about Google Fiber Coming to Your Town

HEALTH

Is Too Much Tanning a Mental Illness?

4 Diet Secrets of the U.S. Olympics Women's Hockey Team

The Internet is a Safer Place for Your Teen Than You Think

TECH

Facebook's WhatsApp Acquisition Explained

Microsoft Stops Hiding Office's Free Online Edition

The Thiel Launch Trailer Has Everything, Including Electric Guitars

ENTERTAINMENT

Beloved TV Show *Pushing Daisies* May Become A Broadway Musical

Lorde's Collaboration With Disclosure Has Given Us the Best "Royals" Remix Yet

Kanye West, Elton John, Skrillex to Perform at Bonnaroo 2014 (Probably Not All At Once)

PHOTOGRAPHY

MAGAZINE

🔊 Empty Slopes

🔊 Joel Stein: DNA of Champions

🔊 The Tonight Show's Upworthy New Host

🔊 Frozen's Hot Following

Center Column

The Magazine Subscribe

The Strange World of Airline Cancellations

Party Foul in U.S. Politics

A Step Backward for Labor

Young Kids, Old Bodies

Table of Contents

Subscribe Now

Online Issue Archive

Facebook Snags WhatsApp in Its Biggest Buy Yet

Social networking giant purchases the global messaging app for $19 billion

- Facebook Rejected WhatsApp Founder For a Job in 2009
- Report: Google Also Wanted WhatsApp With $10 Billion Bid

DON'T MISS

Fire Forces Evacuation of Iowa Town
Responders battle blaze at nearby fertilizer plant

Kansas Spanking Bill Gets Spanked
It would've permitted up to 10 strikes on a child's behind

Obama, Canadian Prime Minister in Beer Bet
The real question is what kind of brew is at stake

CEO Gives Harvard $150 Million
Hedge-fund head offers largest gift ever

Alaska's Road From Nowhere
Government rejects gravel path, leading to deadly problem

***Gravity* Won't Win Best Picture**
Corliss on the cinematic glory that will doom it

New *Fantastic Four* Finds Its Superheroes
But none of the stars are household names

Latest Headlines

- Pope Francis Meets With Prisoners at His Home
- 27 Liberal Groups Oppose Obama Judicial Nominee
- One Californian Won the $425 Million Powerball
- Bitcoin ATM Arrives at Boston Rail Hub
- Natural Gas Prices Surge to a 5-Year High
- Miami Dolphins Fire Coach After Harassment Report
- Idaho Couples Sue to Overturn Gay Marriage Ban
- 4 Accused of Cutting Swastika Into Classmate's Head
- Tearful Korean Reunions Begin; First Since 2010
- CNN: Where the Middle Class Thrives

Editor's Picks On Weather.Com

London's River Thames Breaches Banks

America's Best Winter Drives

Winter Storm Pax Forecast: Southern Snow and Ice

Most Read | Most Emailed

1. Russian Figure Skater Takes a Fall, and More Surprises from the Ladies Short Program
2. Tales from the TSA: Confiscating Aluminum Foil and Watching Out for Solar Powered Bombs
3. Soda Wars Bubble Up Across the Country
4. Alaskan Outrage As Obama Appointee Rejects Wilderness Road
5. Two Americans Found Dead on 'Captain Phillips' Ship
6. The One Word You Need to Stop Using Immediately
7. Britney Spears Forgot to Lip Sync During Her Las Vegas Show, But That's Okay
8. Now There's Another Reason Sitting Will Kill You
9. The New <i>Fantastic Four</i> Has Found Its Superheroes
10. Here's Why Your Netflix Is Slowing Down

Person Of The Year

The People's Pope
He took the name of a humble saint and then called for a church of healing. Read more about Pope Francis and see the rest of the shortlist.

Right Screenshot (Mobile)

TIME

Follow Apps

SECTIONS ▸

■ Al-Jazeera journalists trial starts in Eg...

Bulent Kilic / AFP / Getty Images

Allies Abandon Ukraine Leader

By Simon Shuster / Kiev

The nation's embattled President finds his inner circle becoming increasingly smaller as the revolution's death toll climbs

- E.U. Imposes Sanctions on Ukrainian Officials
- Battleground Kiev: 'Halfway Between a War and A Protest'
- Ukraine Inches Ever Closer to a Full-Blown Civil War
- Ukrainian Skier Withdraws From Olympics to Protest at Home

Facebook Snags WhatsApp in Its Biggest Buy Yet

- Facebook Rejected WhatsApp Founder For a Job in 2009
- Report: Google Also Wanted WhatsApp With $10 Billion Bid

2 Americans Found Dead on *Captain Phillips* Ship

Pussy Riot Releases Music Video of Sochi Beating

DON'T MISS

Fire Forces Evacuation of Iowa Town
Responders battle blaze at nearby fertilizer plant

Kansas Spanking Bill Gets Spanked
It would've permitted up to 10 strikes on a child's behind

Obama, Canadian Prime Minister in Beer Bet
The real question is what kind of brew is at stake

CEO Gives Harvard $150 Million
Hedge-fund head offers largest gift ever

Alaska's Road From Nowhere
Government rejects gravel path, leading to deadly problem

***Gravity* Won't Win Best Picture**
Corliss on the cinematic glory that will doom it

New *Fantastic Four* Finds Its Superheroes
But none of the stars are household names

VIDEO

▶ Kiev's Frontline From Instagram: A View From The Ground

▶ 'The Lego Movie' Animators Show How the Film Was Made

▶ Korean Families Reunite After 60 Years of Separation

Responsive design is **much more** than the simple re-arrangement or stacking of content "blocks"

Therefore, designers need to create three individual, yet related, grid systems for a single page layout.

For **desktop** (over 768 pixels wide), a common grid for design purposes is sized between 950 pixels and 990 pixels wide, but it can be up to 1,200 pixels as monitor resolutions continue to increase. Once the width has been determined, a designer decides how many columns are needed. More columns means more design flexibility; however, too many columns can make recognizing relationships difficult. There is no right number of columns, but the optimal grid gives a layout a clear sense of organization while still allowing for flexibility. The column width for a grid is determined by the overall width divided by the number of columns. And finally, gutters, or the spaces between the columns, are added, providing separation between the elements in each column.

A **tablet** layout (less than 768 but more than 480) shares many relationships to the desktop grid. Generally, the number of columns would be reduced by half and the gutter widths decrease slightly. Often, designers will remove the margin, or space surrounding the page, including a background image or pattern, to maximize the useable space.

Finally, a **mobile** grid (less than 480 pixels wide) is reduced to a single column. Given the narrowness of the screen, more than one—or possibly two—columns causes issues of legibility and usability as design elements, including buttons, get smaller. Often the navigation changes to a drop-down menu and much of the imagery is removed from the page by the CSS to conserve download times.

Desktop > 768 pixels wide

Tablet < 768 pixels but > 480 pixesl wide

Mobile < 480 pixesl

Responsive design **fluidly responds** to the width of a browser. Adaptive design generally has two to four **pre-formatted design states**.

Responsive vs. Adaptive Layouts

Often mistakenly used interchangeably, responsive and adaptive design are slightly different. Responsive design fluidly responds to the width of a browser, forming a clear layout at any width between 480 pixels and more than 768 pixels. Adaptive design generally has two to four pre-formatted design states that it "snaps" to depending on the width of the browser. This offers a designer a bit more control over the layout as there are no in-between sizes that can sometimes produce visually awkward layouts. While it is more common to produce a responsive design, adaptive design can be very useful, especially if the target user group is small and its technology is well defined.

(Opposite) Carters.com, the children's clothing store, takes a unique approach to their mobile site. Much of the content from the desktop site is stripped away in lieu of navigation. This is done for two reasons: to help with the speed of the download of each page (saving data charges for the user); and to expedite the shopping process.

Connect with *your* MICA. *Find information for:*

Students • Faculty • Staff • Alumni • Parents • Employers   LOGIN »

ONLINE GALLERY
See more current work by students, faculty, and alumni »

M|C|A
MARYLAND INSTITUTE COLLEGE OF ART

- About MICA
- Research at MICA
- Admission & Financial Aid
- Programs of Study
- Academic Services & Libraries
- Campus & Student Life

Events & Exhibitions
News
Browse Art
Calendar
Give to MICA

SEARCH

NEWS

LEADING THE WORLD OF VISUAL ART

Joan Waltemath Named Director of Hoffberger School of Painting

THE SECOND-EVER FULLTIME HEAD OF PRESTIGIOUS M.F.A. PROGRAM TAKES REINS AUG. 1

Joan Waltemath will be the second permanent director of the famed Hoffberger School of Painting. Led for more than 40 years by Grace Hartigan until her death in 2008, the M.F.A. program is noted for producing generations of painters who have had an impact in the art world.

Three From MICA Community Receive Notification of Fulbright Scholarships

AWARDS ARE FOR PROPOSALS TO INDIA, TURKEY AND THE CZECH REPUBLIC

Jenny Mullins '09 (Hoffberger School of Painting), Ellye Bloom '10 (printmaking) and photography faculty member Lynn Silverman have all received notification of winning Fulbright Scholarships for the 2010-11 year.

EVENTS & EXHIBITIONS

Commencement Weekend Offers Exhibition, Art Sales, May 13–17

THE WEEKEND INCLUDES THE 2010 COMMENCEMENT EXHIBITION, ARTWALK AND THE MICA MASTERS BENEFIT ART SALE

MICA celebrates its 160st Commencement with a weekend of arts-related events and exhibitions that invite the community to the College.

Contemporary Museum, MICA Organize McCallum and Tarry Survey, May 8–July 31

EXHIBITION PREMIERES THE ARTISTS' In 'PROJECTION SERIES,' AT THE CONTEMPORARY MUSEUM

▶ LISTEN   ▶ WATCH

the first large-scale survey of Bradley McCallum and Jacqueline Tarry, the exhibition premieres the artists' 'Projection Series,' at the Contemporary Museum, May 8–July 31. Earlier site-specific projects will be exhibited throughout Baltimore.

STUDENT, FACULTY & ALUMNI NEWS

Books, Publications Created by Alumni, Faculty, Students

READING MATERIAL PRODUCED BY THE MICA COMMUNITY

Overview in chronological order of books and articles published or designed by members of the MICA community in 2010. Including, Mina Cheon will read from and sign her book, Shamanism + Cyberspace, May 19 in New York City.

MICA Presents an Exhibition Celebrating the Beauty of Rochefort-en-Terre, May 29–June 20

NINETEEN ARTISTS HIGHLIGHT THE 'MAGIC' OF BRITTANY, FRANCE

MICA presents an exhibition highlighting the work of 19 alumni and faculty who have been inspired by their participation in MICA's celebrated artist-in-residency program. "MICA@Rochefort-en-Terre: MICA Artists, Rochefort Alumni" is on view Saturday, May 29-Sunday, June 20, with a reception on Tuesday, June 8, 5:30-7 p.m., in the Fox Building's Meyerhoff and Decker galleries.

Two Alumni Compete on New Bravo Series

MARK YOUR CALENDARS: THE FIRST EPISODE OF THIS NEW REALITY COMPETITION AIRS JUNE 9

John Parot '98 and Jaclyn Santos '07 are two of 14 contestants competing in "Work of Art: The Next Great Artist," Bravo's latest incarnation of reality competitions that pits artist against artist.

▶ WATCH

May Boasts Many Off-Campus Exhibitions, Events Featuring Alumni, Faculty, Students

MONTHLY HIGHLIGHTS OF MICA COMMUNITY EXHIBITIONS, INSTALLATIONS

Ongoing list of members of the MICA community who have their work featured in shows, lectures off-campus in May.

Section II

DESIGN

CHAPTER 4

ANATOMY OF A WEB PAGE

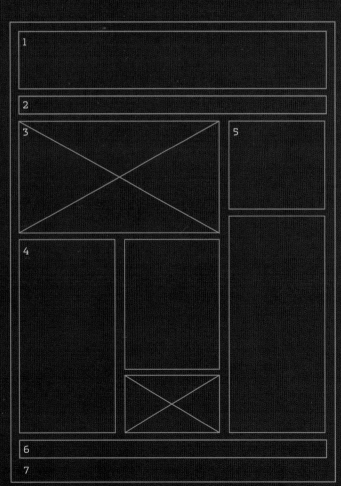

1. Header
2. Navigation
3. Feature
4. Body/Content
5. Sidebar
6. Footer
7. Background

Form & Function of Web Design

Web design, like any other form of design, requires the designer to understand the end user's habits, the context in which the work is received, and the necessary function of the end product. These factors usually present limitations that set the boundaries for starting a design project. For Web design, these boundaries have caused several design and structural conventions to emerge. Such conventions include a page header, persistent navigation, content areas and sidebars, footer navigation, and often a background treatment. Although styling and aesthetics vary greatly from site to site, most sites adhere to this basic structure. Each of these common Web design elements, and their placement on the page, came to be for several basic reasons.

THE NATURE OF HOW THE PAGES ARE VIEWED

In Western culture, we're conditioned to read from left to right, top to bottom. Therefore, the natural position for important information would be the upper left of a Web page. This ensures that elements such as logos, navigation, and "featured items" are perceived first by the user.

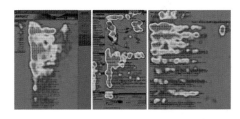

These images show the results of an eye-tracking study. They indicate that users focus their attention on the upper-left area of a Web page.

The notion that users scan pages from left to right, top to bottom, has been validated through the use of eye tracking studies. Sophisticated cameras fixed to the top of a computer screen have the ability to track the eye movements of Internet users and map out the patterns. The red areas in the images below indicate where users focused most of their attention. They reveal not only the fact that users' attention is mainly focused on the upper left of a page, but also that Web users skim a page for key points, as shown by the spotty bits of color in the center and left images.

Many Web design conventions are borrowed from the world of print communication. Pictured here is the New York Times newspaper showing a header and feature area very similar to those on a Web page.

The "fold"

BORROWED CONVENTIONS

Because almost all early Web designers were amateur designers or trained as print designers, elements from print design were converted to Web design. Design elements like headers, feature areas, body text, and sidebars all come directly from age-old newspaper design standards.

The "fold" of a newspaper is literally the horizontal crease in the center of the front page delineating the top half from the bottom half. Newspaper editors tend to put as much of the most important information as possible above that fold since that's the area that potential newspaper buyers will see. Similarly, a "fold" on a Web page is the line that delineates where the browser window cuts off the content. Areas above the fold are seen by the user when the page loads. Content below the fold requires that users scroll down.

USER EXPECTATIONS

Sites that want to attract the masses, like news portals, travel sites, e-commerce sites, etc., need to appeal to the lowest common denominator in terms of one's ability to use technology. As the Web became established in the mid- to late 1990s, companies interested in having their users find what they wanted quickly would imitate the metaphors for navigation and site layout from other, already established, sites. For example, Amazon.com is credited with creating the first tab-style navigation (another borrowed convention); although there are probably earlier examples, the "tabs" served as a metaphor that worked in part because tabs were something people understood from the "real world" of file folders. As a result, Web sites all over the Internet began using a tab structure for their navigation—and still do to this day. Even Apple.com, known widely for its innovative design, once used a tabbed navigation very similar to that of Amazon.

Image of Apple.com from 2007 showing the tabbed navigation style.

At the height of the tab craze in 2000, some said that the navigation on Amazon.com resembled a graveyard.

SEARCH ENGINE OPTIMIZATION (SEO)

Having a high search engine rank is critical to a company's online success. A higher rank on a list of search results means more traffic. Search engines, such as Google.com and Bing.com, use various methods to evaluate the content of a site and determine its rank. Some design factors that influence the search engine optimization of a page include: text links in the main navigation; multiple keyword-rich text links throughout the page; limited use of images, especially images of text, since search engines cannot get content from images; bolded subhead copy styled with the <H> tags; and important content placed above the fold—the higher the better. Although these are not all of the SEO factors that influence the rank of a page, these are generally the factors that a designer has the most control over. The topic of SEO is discussed further in chapter 7.

Orbitz.com is a good example of a page designed for SEO. Multiple keyword-rich text links, bolded subheads, and limited use of imagery consistently produce a top ranking for searches of "Vacation Packages."

ADVERTISING STANDARDS

The Interactive Advertising Bureau (IAB) was established in 1996 to set up standard practices in Web advertising. The organization sets forth rules that govern the size, shape, and file weight (among other things) for advertising assets. This helps advertisers create a finite series of banners that can be used on any Web site that adopts the IAB standards. For Web designers, this means that their Web design must accommodate banners that are 300 x 250 pixels ("big box"), 180 x 600 pixels ("skyscraper"), and/or 728 x 90 pixels ("leaderboard"), among others. If a Web site is funded with ad revenue, these dimensions become a critical part of the framework of the site. Additionally, advertisers want their ads above the fold so that the user sees them immediately. Web site owners, on the other hand, don't want the ads to overpower the message of the site. Web designers satisfy both sides by establishing a structure that flows with the required sizes of the ads—a 300-pixel-wide sidebar will fit a big box ad without any dead space around it, for example.

Yahoo.com and many other sites across the Web display advertising. In this example of the home page, a "big box" ad appears in the right-hand sidebar. The sidebar for this page has been designed to accommodate a banner having a standard width of 300 pixels.

Without **understanding the function** behind standard Web design conventions, designers are purely imitating things that they've seen.

While these particular factors are unique to Web design, the idea of a set of parameters that restrict and inform a design is not unique. Car designers, for example, are faced with hundreds, if not thousands, of these types of challenges. People want to be able to drive more than one make of car without having to work to relocate and decipher the speedometer, for instance. Yet, there's a wide range of variation in the sizes and shapes of cars on the road today.

The duality of form and function is a universal design concept; however, most new Web designers aren't as aware as they should be of the technical and functional implications behind the design decisions they make. Without understanding the function behind standard Web design conventions, designers are purely imitating things that they've seen. This chapter explores the parts of a Web page and specifically how those parts contribute to the overall effectiveness of a site—aesthetically and technically.

Car designers face similar challenges as Web designers when designing a dashboard interface. They seek a balance between unique style and standardization and ease of use.

Beyond Conventional

This chapter examines the structural design conventions that have evolved to make up Web pages. This idea is different than the concept of design templates or "themes" that have become very common with the emergence of content management systems (CMS) like WordPress and Drupal. Below are the "Church Theme" and the "Lifestyle Theme" designed by StudioPress for use with WordPress. Notice how they are identical in structure and format. The only difference between the two is their "skin"—the colors, fonts, and images. While theme-based Web design makes having a Web site easy and affordable, the concept has the potential to erode the value of what Web designers do. At worst, it turns design and creativity into a commodity and homogenizes the look of the Web.

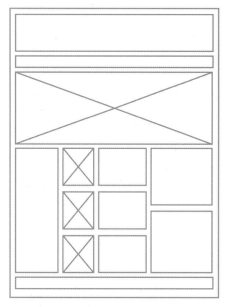

MarthaStewart.com is an elegant design example from both a structural as well as an aesthetic point of view. The subtle and consistent design treatments give the site a uniquely Martha Stewart feel, despite using a standard Web structure.

The header graphic for GQ.com uses the magazine's iconic logo as the central element. The clean, centered design approach creates a unique and identifiable presence for the brand.

Header

The header of a Web page is one area that remains relatively consistent throughout a Web site. It acts as a grounding force for the user by identifying and visually unifying all the pages of a site. Headers establish the brand look and feel for a site and often will present the user with a call to action—search, buy, register, etc. The header of a page must perform these tasks without overpowering the content of the page and distracting the user.

Because the header area tends to stay consistent from page to page, it is often where the client's logo appears. It has become a common expectation of users that the logo on a site, specifically one located in the header of a page, will link the user back to the home page.

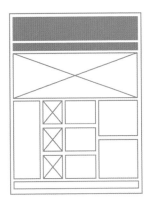

Headers act as a grounding force for the user by **identifying** and **visually unifying** all the pages of a site.

The code behind the header contains information that is vital to the search engine optimization of the page. From metadata (keywords and descriptions of the page in the code) to the page title (this is the line of copy that appears on the top of a browser window), search engines use these elements to begin indexing the content of the page.

The header on 99u.com is a fixed, or "sticky," header that does not scroll with the page. In its initial state, the header takes up a good amount of space to accomodate the logo, tagline, social links, and a search feature. As the page scrolls (bottom), the navigation slides over, and the logo appears in the black bar. This is useful for long pages as it gives users access to the navigation, even in the middle of the page.

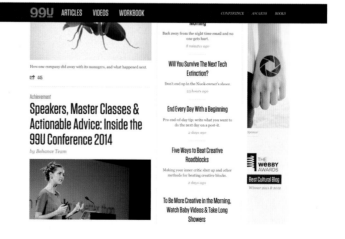

CNN.com's bold use of their brand color and centered placement of their logo make for a distinctive page header.

Staples.com is an example of an extremely functional header. The logo is flanked by shopping tools like the search bar and the shopping cart.

Navigation

Often included in the header of a Web page is the navigation, or menu, of pages available on a site. The navigation should stand apart from the page visually and appear in some way to be clickable (or tappable in the case of mobile). As discussed in the previous chapter, navigation is an essential part of the usability of a site, therefore the button labeling should be clear and legible.

Often, there is a need to break up the navigation into primary and secondary navigation areas. The primary navigation should lead to the pages most useful to the users and the labels should clearly and concisely convey the content they lead to. The secondary navigation usually contains things like company info, contact information, and possibly a link to a blog or other secondary items. This division not only helps with the usability of a site but it also helps create a sense of visual organization and hierarchy on a page.

The heavily stylized drop-down menu on this site helps it fit in with the rest of the site design.

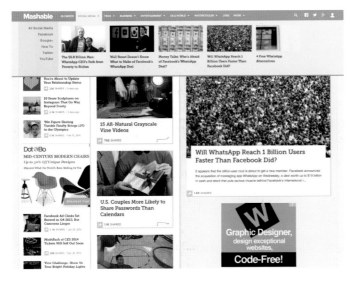

Mashable.com has an elegant drop-down system that presents the user with photos for the key stories, attracting them to the content.

Navigation can be horizontal along the top of a page or vertical along the side of a page, or even a combination of the two. Navigational elements are also contained in the footer of a page, which is discussed later in this chapter.

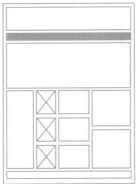

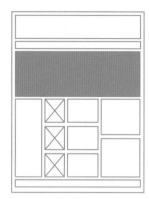

Feature Area

One indication of effective design is a clearly defined hierarchy of information. To achieve this, designers use a focal point—an area in the composition that is perceived before all others and serves as an entry point into the layout. In Web design this is often the main feature area. This area usually takes up a large portion of the home page, has the most vibrant color and typography, and usually features some sort of motion or animation. All of these things combine to make it the most important visual item on the page.

The most common option for a feature area is a slideshow of imagery and content from the site. This can be achieved using SEO-friendly technology like JavaScript and Ajax. Adobe Flash can also be used for highly interactive feature areas or ones that involve sophisticated animation.

MarthaStewart.com has a tasteful feature slideshow that highlights various content from the site with each frame indicated by a tab at the bottom. This solution also includes a pause/play button so users can stop the animation, reducing distractions as they read other content on the page.

To achieve hierarchy, designers use a
focal point—an area in the composition
that is perceived before all others.

Apple.com uses the feature area to highlight
their latest products. Dramatic photos
combined with simple, pithy headlines set in
minimalist typography result in an impactful
presentation with a clear focal point and call
to action.

The feature area on Disney.com extends beyond the confines of the box in which it is contained. The background color changes based on the content of the "slide," giving the entire page a unique feel with every change.

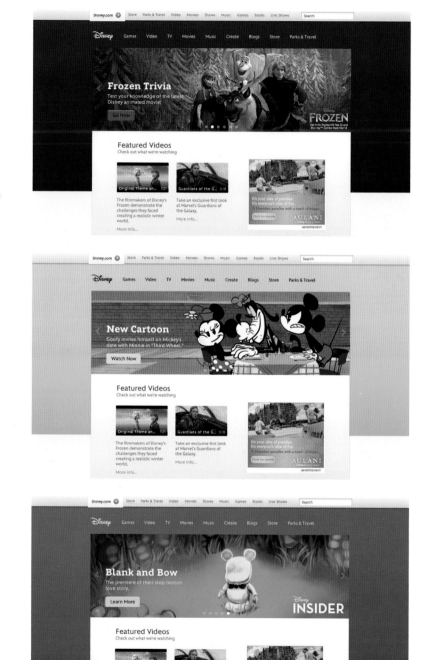

The feature area of a Web page doesn't need to be boxed in. This stunning example from EA.com blurs the lines between a feature area and a background image.

Breaks in the content allow users to scan the layout quickly and give them **multiple entry points** into the page.

Body/Content

The body or content area of a Web site is where users spend most of their time, as it usually represents the end of their search for content. This is where traditional design ideas of legibility and clarity come into play, but with some added considerations. A Web page can be any height, however, it is always seen through a window, the size of which is determined by the user's settings. The area of a page that users first see in their browser window when a page loads is the area known to be above the fold. The content in this area must quickly convey the nature of the content that appears outside of that area, known as below the fold. Telegraphing the content on a page with clear and descriptive headlines as well as appropriate imagery is not the same as delivering all of the content above the fold. Users have become accustomed to scrolling down a page in order to reveal more content, just as newspaper readers will leaf through a paper as a story progresses.

It's important to break up long stretches of content with white space and clearly identifiable subheadings. These breaks in the content allow users to skim the page quickly, and it gives them multiple entry points into the content. Dividing up the content by using heading tags (<H1>, <H2>, and so on) helps search engines evaluate the content of a page. Some search engines place a higher value on words contained within these tags, since they tend to summarize the key points from the content. Learn more about SEO in chapter 7.

Energy Efficiency
iMac is designed to be energy efficient right out of the box. It has even earned the EPA's ENERGY STAR qualification for its low power consumption.

Efficient power supply.
iMac includes a highly efficient power supply that reduces the amount of power wasted when bringing electricity from the wall to your computer. Lower power consumption reduces energy bills and lessens the environmental impact of greenhouse gas emissions from power plants.

Advanced power management.
Unlike a lot of Windows–based PC systems, iMac uses energy-efficient hardware components that work hand in hand with the operating system to conserve power. Mac OS X spins down hard drives and activates sleep mode on already energy-efficient LED-backlit displays. And it balances tasks across both central processors and graphics processors. Mac OS X never misses a power-saving opportunity, no matter how small. It even regulates the processor between keystrokes, reducing power between the letters you type. That's just one of many ways Apple manages small amounts of power that add up to big savings.

ENERGY STAR qualification.
iMac meets the stringent low power requirements set by the EPA, giving it ENERGY STAR qualification. ENERGY STAR 5.0 sets significantly higher efficiency limits for power supplies and aggressive limits for the computer's typical annual power consumption.

Eliminating Toxic Substances
It's what iMac doesn't have that makes it more environmentally friendly. It's free of many harmful toxins, including mercury, arsenic, BFRs, and PVC.

Fewer toxins.
The greatest environmental challenge facing the computer industry is the presence of arsenic, brominated flame retardants (BFRs), mercury, phthalates, and polyvinyl chloride (PVC) in products. Apple engineers have worked hard to eliminate BFRs and PVC from iMac circuit boards, internal and external cables, connectors, insulators, adhesives, and more.[2] And they've eliminated many other toxins that are a common part of desktop computer manufacturing — choosing, for example, mercury–free backlighting and arsenic–free glass for the iMac display.

Recyclability
Because iMac is made from materials such as aluminum and glass, it's more likely to be recycled and reused at the end of its long, productive life.

Recyclable materials.
Apple designers and engineers have integrated the entire iMac computer into an enclosure made from a single, solid piece of recyclable aluminum. The display is made of recyclable glass. Both the aluminum and glass materials are very desirable to recyclers, which means the raw materials used in iMac can be reused in other products.

Free recycling for your old computer.
If you live in the U.S., Apple offers a free recycling program for old computers and displays with the purchase of any new Mac. Learn more on the Apple Recycling site ▸

EPEAT Gold
iMac has earned EPEAT Gold[3] status for its responsible manufacture, energy efficiency, and recyclability.

The EPEAT Gold rating.
Through its innovative and environmentally friendly design, iMac has earned the highest rating of EPEAT Gold[3]. The Electronic Product Environmental Assessment Tool, or EPEAT, evaluates the environmental impact of a product based on how recyclable it is, how much energy it uses, and how it's designed and manufactured.

Bolded subheads, iconography, and generous white space make this page from Apple.com easy to scan to find the information you're looking for.

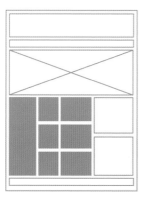

Linked words within the text of a page help to organize ideas and reduce the need for long pages; if a user would like to know more about a related topic, the user can click to another page rather than have all the information on a single page.

Highlighted text links on both GapersBlock.com and AndyRutledge.com help the user scan for related information and key ideas contained within the linked text.

The **optimal line length** for ideal legibility is no more than two to two and a half alphabets—52 to 65 characters.

In addition to not having a height limit, Web pages also don't have a limit to how wide they can be. Web designers have two options for addressing the problem of page width variability. Most current sites have a fixed width frame or boundary, whereas the content is confined to a box with a set size that floats in the browser window as it expands and contracts. The second option is to have variable-width columns. Variable-width layouts were popular in early Web design primarily because they were easy to produce. Designers would simply flow copy into a layout, unconcerned with the consequences of expanding browser windows. The issue with variable-width layouts is that without limits to the length of a line of text, it can become illegible. Typographically, the optimal line length for ideal legibility is no more than two to two and a half alphabets—52 to 65 characters. This prevents eye fatigue, both from lines that are too long, where users might lose their place, or lines that are too short, where the user is continually going to the next line after just a word or two.

Jaded zombies
acted quietly but
kept driving their
oxen forward.

Jaded zombies acted quietly but kept driving their oxen forward.
The wizard quickly jinxed the gnomes before they vaporized. All
questions asked by five watched experts amaze the judge. Six boys
guzzled cheap raw plum vodka quite joyfully.

Jaded zombies acted quietly but kept driving their oxen forward. The wizard quickly jinxed the gnomes before they vaporized. All questions asked by five watched experts amaze the judge. Six boys guzzled cheap raw plum vodka quite joyfully. Just keep examining every low bid quoted for zinc etchings. Sixty zippers were quickly picked from the woven jute bag. Few black taxis drive up major roads on quiet hazy nights. Six big devils from Japan quickly forgot how to waltz. Painful zombies quickly watch a jinxed graveyard.

These three examples of text show how a short line length (top) and a long line length (bottom) make text difficult to consume quickly. The middle example contains 52 to 65 characters in a single line, presenting optimal legibility.

Wikipedia.org uses a variable width for the body/content area of the page. Both of these images are of the same page, showing a narrow browser window and a very wide window.

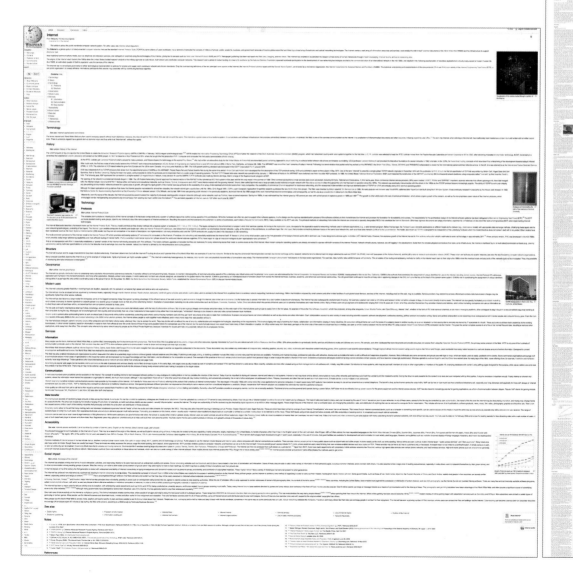

Sidebar

The sidebar of a Web page contains secondary information that either supports the main content of the page or directs users to related content through the use of submenus and links. Areas of a sidebar are often sold for advertising space. Skyscrapers and Big Box ads, as they are known in the online media industry, typically fit well within the modular structure of a sidebar. As with the header, the design of a sidebar should blend in with the look of the site so as not to visually overshadow the content of the page, helping to create an overall feel for the page.

Sidebars, like the ones shown here from Kinder-Aktuell.de (above) and Breez.com.au (right), are useful for providing supporting information as well as advertising space.

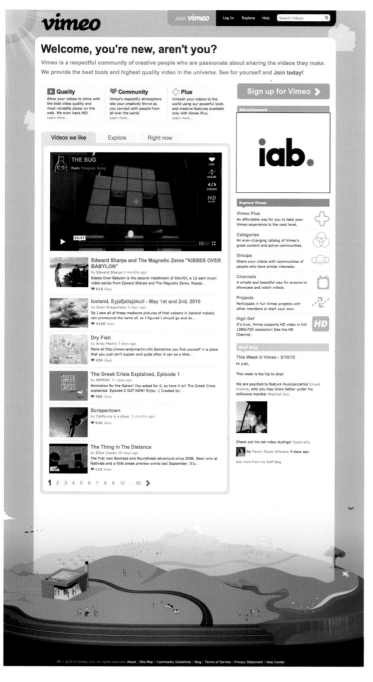

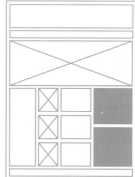

The sidebar on Vimeo.com begins with a call to action for new users to sign up. The 300-pixel-wide column also has space for standard IAB ads and related item links, each color coded for increased usability.

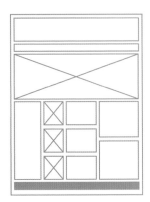

Footer

The footer, or the very bottom of a Web page, is a critical part of Web design, performing tasks for both the user and search engine optimization. In the early days of Web design, the footer would contain the copyright information for the site as well as a couple of links. Over time, Web page footers have grown to resemble a mini–site map, with links to each of the main pages of the site. These links not only help the user navigate the site but also help search engines like Google index the site properly, improving the search engine ranking—Google places a higher value on words contained within links.

Technically, the footer of a Web site contains much of the specialized coding for the page like page-tracking code or lengthy JavaScript functions. This is again due to SEO. Long bits of copy at the top of a page will push the important information down farther. Google places a higher value on information that's higher up on a page.

The footer for GQ.fr houses all of the related information that a reader could need — from subscription and app downloads, to social media and contact information.

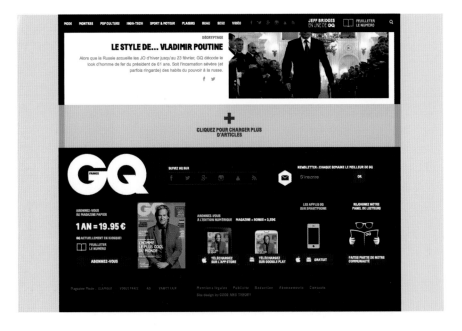

The footer of automaker Honda.com gives a complete list of areas of the site and also adds a small bit of visual interest with a randomly appearing image.

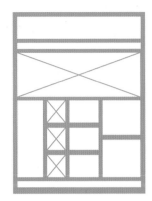

Background

In the earliest days of Web design, designers would use a repeating graphic in the background of a Web page, imitating the effect of patterned wallpaper. Today, thanks to increased bandwidth and faster connection speeds, Web page backgrounds are used in bolder and more sophisticated ways to complement the content of the page. Backgrounds can be used to create depth or dimension, add richness with texture and color, or even expand the content beyond the borders of the page.

The designers of Vaseline.com turned the background into a critical element of the page. Large images of smooth skin lie beneath a simple CSS design structure.

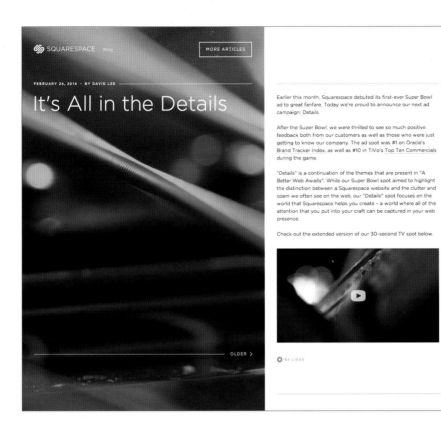

The large background images on SquareSpace.com integrate with the content and give added detail to the posts.

Wiski.com uses a topographical map in the background, which also gives the user a feeling of snow.

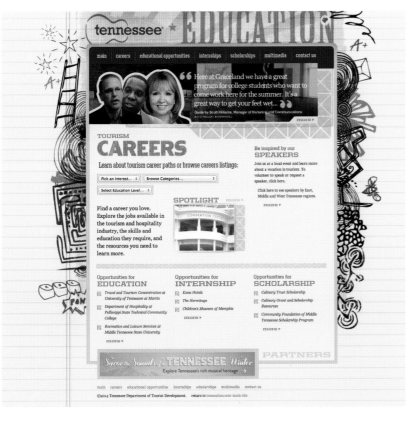

The background of a Web page doesn't need to recede or be subordinate, as seen in these examples, both from Tennessee. The illustration in the background of these pages adds both visual interest and content to the page.

The background images on en.opera.se give a dramatic sense to the pages of the site because of their contrast of scale.

The dark wood panel pattern in the background of these sites gives the pages texture and creates a mood that's dark, rugged, natural, and masculine.

There is some debate between Web designers and usability experts regarding the use of dark background and light text. Most experts believe that it's more difficult to read light text that's reversed out of a dark background; however, many designers prefer the look of dark backgrounds. As with many other decisions a Web designer makes, this one comes down to the tolerance and preference of the user.

Blackle.com, a Web site that employs the Google Custom Search tool, mimics Google.com but with a black background. The site, created by Heap Media, claims to save energy by reducing the amount of watts a monitor needs to display black versus white.

CHAPTER 5

THE ELEMENTS OF WEB DESIGN

Creating a design system so that dissimilar types of content appear to work together is what graphic designers have been doing for centuries, and Web design is no different. The previous chapter explored various structural and spatial methods of organizing space and creating a structure. Design is about more than simply organizing information, however; it's about making something distinctive and memorable. This chapter explores the aesthetic treatment of the elements within a design that not only help form relationships within a system but create a visual style.

Web Design Style

A design style is an attempt at connecting with a user's sensibilities and a basic need to relate to things. The elements of a design style include color, texture, typography, and imagery use. Additionally, there are means of manipulating these elements, including creating a sense of scale or depth, animation, and variation. The crafting and manipulation of these aesthetic elements of style make a particular design unique and, better yet, memorable.

In all forms of design, a style comes primarily from two areas: the trends of the time—what's fashionable—and the technology that's available to create a piece of design. Graphic design, which dates back to cave paintings and carries on through the carved letterforms on Trajan's column, handwritten manuscripts, Gutenberg's movable type, right on through to photo reproduction and the modern computer age, has always been heavily influenced by the technology available to produce it.

The same is true in Web design. As computer technology, browsing software, and the markup language that makes up a design become more advanced, they influence the design styles and trends. Through it all, however, great design is defined by the fundamental understanding of the hierarchical structure that makes up a layout, explored in the previous chapter, combined with the elements of style that give a design its uniqueness.

This page from the Gutenberg Bible, the first Western example of movable-type printing, represented state-of-the-art technology when it was produced in the 1450s.

Color

More than any other design element, color has the ability to guide, direct, and persuade a user. In addition to its instructive qualities, color can appeal to a user's emotions by setting a mood or a tone for a piece of design. Colors signify meaning for many people and cultures, making it a powerful tool for designers. The immediacy with which color can be recognized makes it valuable for forming clear relationships.

Color has three main properties: hue, which is commonly known as the color; value, which is the darkness or lightness; and saturation, which is the vibrancy of a color. Because Web design is based on the colors of light (red, blue, and green), the range of colors is greater than with print design, which uses the reflective palette (cyan, magenta, yellow, and black). Although there's a broader color palette, predicting the exact color a user sees is difficult because of variations among monitors and operating systems.

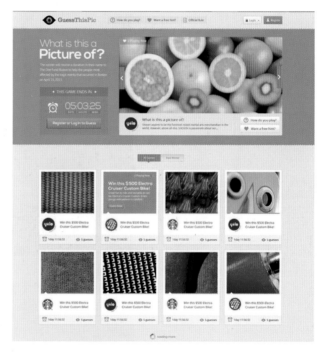

Sometimes limiting the number of colors used in a layout can have a big impact. The use of yellow in the navigation, design elements and photography helps Meacuppa.be create a strong and memorable visual identity.

Relationships of color help users create associations among otherwise unrelated elements within a design.

Color is an excellent way to create relationships within a design. USAToday.com uses colored type to signify various categories; blue for news, red for sports, purple for life, green for money, etc. This use of color helps users quickly scan a page to find information without the need for a lot of reading.

Contrasting color can help a designer guide and direct a user through a layout.

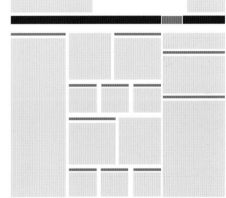

Effectively using color doesn't necessarily mean creating a colorful design. This example, NewYorkMag.com, uses only touches of red among a sea of black and white to lead the user and highlight key information. The schematic (above right) illustrates how color guides the eye down and around the page.

Texture

Adding texture to a Web design gives the user sense of a tactile experience and helps connect him or her to the content of a page. Types of texture can range from smooth, shiny buttons that are common in Web 2.0 design, to rough or grungy treatments, to type imagery or backgrounds. Aside from the stylistic treatments of texture, it's important to remember that on a macro level, every design has a texture, intended or not. Type, images, and illustrations combine to make an overall texture that the user perceives on a subconscious level.

LeadersTheConference.com employs an overall texture that gives the page a unique feel that pulls the user in and unifies the overall look.

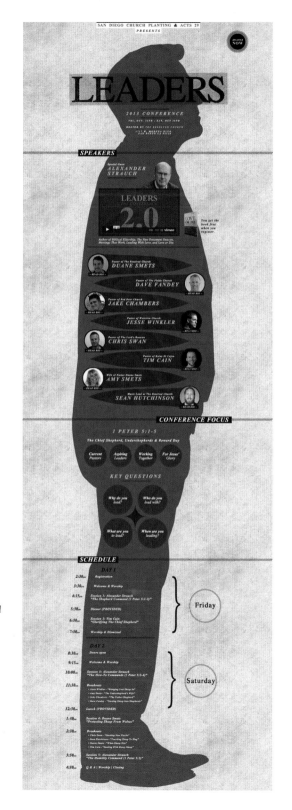

Adding texture to a Web design gives the user the sense of a **tactile experience** and helps connect him or her to the content of a page.`

The stucco texture on Jarritos.com comes from the Mexican theme that permeates the site.

Handiemail.com uses a subtle paper texture to enhance the concept of hand-written letters made from emails.

Imagery & Iconography

Studies show that users don't read Web sites, they scan them. For Web designers, the use of images or iconography can mean replacing wordy descriptions with single images, making a layout easier for a user to get information from quickly. A designer's choice of imagery should be deliberate and add to either the branding or the message of the page. All images add to a Web page's weight or file size, so gratuitous use of generic imagery can impede a good user experience.

This page for the iMac on Apple.com integrates type and image in such a way that it looks as if the type is wrapping around the image.

See an invisible world.

Measure   Play   Share   Download from the App Store

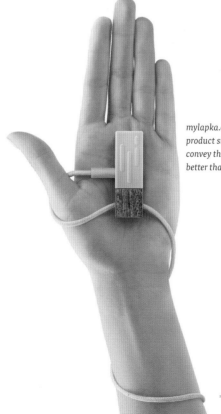

mylapka.com tells an entire brand and product story with imagery. The images convey the features of the product, likely better than paragraphs of copy could.

Ready to explore.

The icons seen here on ThemeKingdom.com help the user quickly scan the content by relating visual elements to the text.

Icons are used in this example to quickly convey the content of the article so users can scan the page and glean a lot of information.

Amplify.

Assessment   Tablet   Curriculum   Services   Viewpoints

Divisions

Amplify comprises three divisions.

The Amplify Insight and Amplify Learning divisions grew out of the work of Wireless Generation and, as a complement, the Amplify Access division was created shortly thereafter. Each of these divisions sells products independently of one another.

Amplify learning.

Amplify insight.   Amplify access.

Amplify insight.

Harnessing the power of data, Amplify Insight's assessment products help teachers assess student progress, respond to individual student needs and accelerate personalized learning. Because achieving personalized learning requires more than technology, Amplify Insight also offers professional and consulting services to support educators and advance their ability to use data to make more effective decisions—from the classroom to the district office.

Amplify learning.

Amplify Learning's curriculum products are reinventing teaching and learning in the core subjects of English Language Arts, math and science. The Amplify Curriculum is written specifically to meet the rigors of the Common Core State Standards, so that students are prepared for college and career success. Amplify Learning's digital curriculum, developed in collaboration with top game designers, academic thought leaders and Hollywood screenwriters, delivers groundbreaking learning experiences that deeply engage students.

Amplify access.

With its tablet-based platform designed specifically for schools, Amplify Access is making one-to-one mobile learning an affordable reality for schools. The Amplify Tablet Package includes intuitive classroom tools and digital educational resources with wireless connectivity and mobile device management. Amplify Access also provides high-quality training, project management and customer support to help ease—and accelerate—a school's transition to mobile-based learning.

Amplify.

Learn about Amplify	Connect with Amplify	Legal
Company	Contact	Terms
Leadership	Support	Privacy
Partners	Events	
Newsroom	Careers	

Keep up with Amplify via Twitter, Facebook, LinkedIn, YouTube, Google+. © 2014 Amplify Education, Inc.

Hand-drawn illustrations combined with photography layered under the content of the page make the side-scrolling site as energetic and dynamic as the music it represents.

Pictured here are three images featuring the iPad from Apple. Each uses scale, but the method of achieving a dramatic sense of scale is slightly different. On the far left, extreme perspective is used to give a sense of depth and make the iPad seem larger than life. In the image on this page, the iPad is the dominant element on the page simply because it's the largest when compared to the other elements. Finally, on the right, the iPads are breaking out of the defined border, making them feel too large to be contained within the space.

Scale

Contrast of size or scale is one way designers can add a sense of drama to a design. Having a dominant element is critical to creating a clear sequence or hierarchy of elements within a design. Scale is a relative design element, so in order to achieve a dynamic feeling of scale, small elements must be included in the layout for comparison's sake. Large design elements that break out of borders or even bleed off the page also heighten the sense of scale.

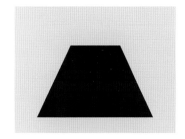

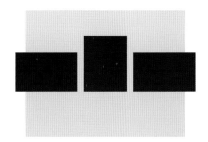

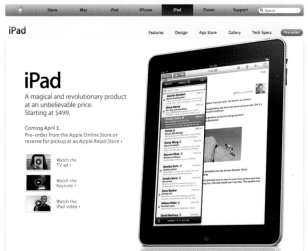

The best way to experience the web, email, photos, and video. Hands down.
Imagine being able to page through websites, write an email, flick through photos, or watch a movie. All on a big, beautiful Multi-Touch screen. With just the touch of a finger. Learn more ›

It's hard to believe we could fit so many great ideas into something so thin.
iPad has a 9.7-inch, LED-backlit IPS display with a remarkably precise Multi-Touch screen. And yet, at just 1.5 pounds and 0.5 inch thin, it's easy to carry and use anywhere. Learn more ›

150,000 apps at your fingertips. From day one.
Right now, iPad can run almost 150,000 of the apps on the App Store. It can even run the apps you've already downloaded for your iPhone or iPod touch. Learn more ›

In this example from FamousCookies.com, the larger-than-life cookies and typography combine with the smaller elements on the page to create a dramatic sense of scale and appetite appeal.

In these examples, JasonSantaMaria.com (top) and TicWatches.com, a dominant design element is used as a focal point to the page. This use of scale pulls the user in, inviting him or her to explore the other elements on the page.

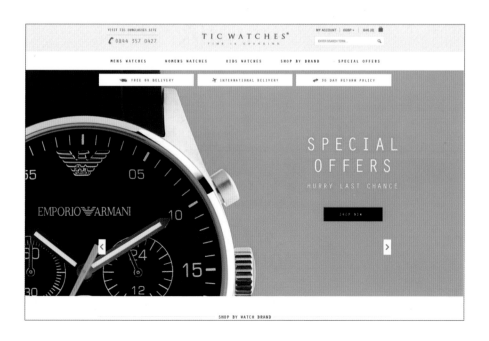

Depth & Dimension

Applying depth and dimension to a page gives it an element of realism, and, like texture, gives the user a more tactile experience. There are many ways to create the illusion of depth in a Web design, like simple overlapping of design elements, adding gradient color and shadows, or even creating three-dimensional elements. Adding depth to a Web page can help add visual interest and draw a user into a design.

This Web page for developer Oliver James Gosling (goslingo.com) gives new meaning to the phrase "above the fold." The subtle gradations of gray and cast shadowing give the appearance of an unfolded brochure.

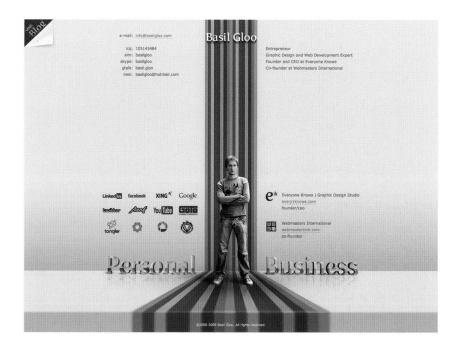

The sites pictured here use color and perspective to create a dynamic and colorful sense of depth. The site above, BasilGloo.com, uses photography and three-dimensional type to create a realistic environment. The site to the left, for Joshua Keckley, uses shadowing and texture to achieve a similar, yet less realistic, effect. Both sites use a focal point to draw the user into the layout.

Adding depth to a Web page can help add **visual interest** and draw a user into a design.

From three-dimensional type and objects in perspective, to layered elements and subtle gradations of color and shadowing, Syfy.com appears to be completely designed around the concept of depth and dimension. Almost every element of the design seems to lift off the screen. The main feature area is a shelf where elements stand, casting a shadow onto the other pieces of information.

PlayMapsCube.com is an extraordinary display of technology to create interactivity, animation, and delight.

Animation

Animation is a tool used by digital designers to layer information, create a sequence of information, or simply surprise and delight the user. Animation can be the focal point of a design—like a slideshow or video in the main feature area—but animation can also be simple and subtle, like small amounts of movement when a user mouses over a button. Too much repetitive animation, especially on pages with a lot of content, can become distracting to a user. Web design best practices dictate that the designer should always give the user the ability to pause a large animation, or, if an animation is looping, to cycle for no more than three cycles.

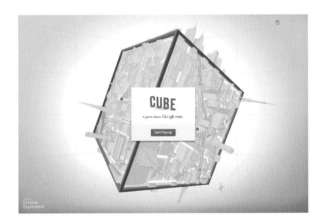

User-initiated animation is a great way to provide feedback or build a story. Animations can be triggered by a user clicking a button or by scrolling down a page. These touches, if used in ways that are true to the client's brand, can really heighten the feeling of an interactive experience rather than a passive one.

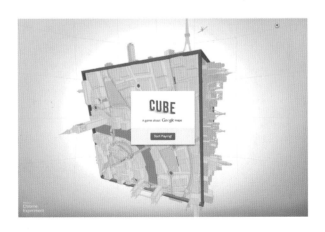

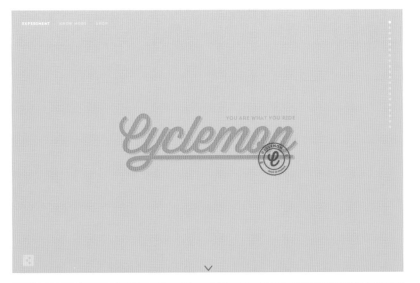

The designers of CyclezMon.com create

Another popular way to add realism and depth to a page is with a parallax scrolling effect. Parallax is a physical phenomenon in which objects that are far way appear to move more slowly than objects that are closer. The parallax technique has been used by makers of cartoons and video games for years. Web designers now use a parallax scrolling effect to add interest and depth to a page.

A stunning and delightful example of scrolling animation is found at WeeSociety.com, designed by the design firm The Office. As the user scrolls down the page, elements animate and build to create colorful and playful vignettes.

This stunning site by Frank Chimero is an outstanding example of the various effects that can be created by parallax scrolling, from multi-part animation at the top, to the illusion of motion pictures in the middle, to more subtle effects at the bottom.

Variability

The speed at which a Web designer can apply changes, combined with the need to continually refresh the look of a site, gives Web designers the ability to vary elements of a design based on things like sections of the site or specific events—or randomly. What was once considered unthinkable—altering a corporate logo, for example—can now be a playful way to add relevance to a Web site. The best way to keep a site fresh is by updating the content. But if that's not possible, design variations can give the user the impression that a site is fresh and current.

The USAToday brand is based on the variable utilization of the circle. Once a globe, it now represents all of the various topics reported by the news company.

The header of the Web site for the American Institute of Graphic Arts features images of design work from their archive. The images randomly appear, giving the site a fresh look each time a user visits the page.

What was once considered to be **unthinkable** can now be a playful way to add relevance and variety.

These images from Google.com show the playfulness with which their designers treat the Google branding, from the anniversary of the moon landing to Dr. Seuss's birthday.

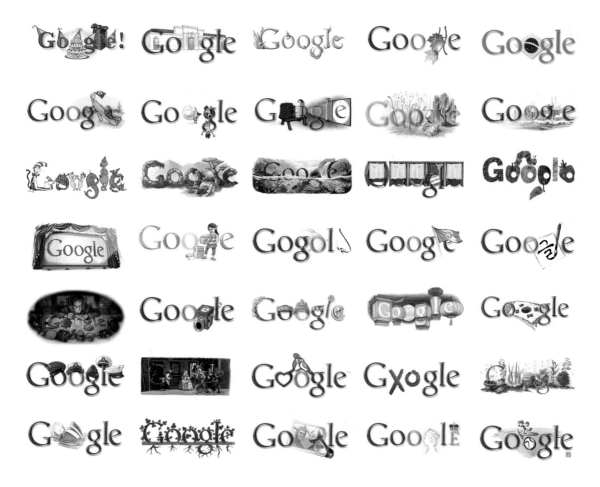

The Web site for the Maryland Institute College of Art, MICA.edu, offers the ability to select from four student project thumbnail images along the top of the page. Each selection completely alters not only the images but the color scheme of the page. The color palette is derived from each piece of student work. In this case, the variability is user-controlled and conceptually it highlights the main constituents of the school: the students.

In this case, the variability is controlled by the user, and conceptually it highlights the main constituents of the school: **the students.**

Modularity

Modularity can mean a couple of things when it comes to Web design. For a Web designer, modularity means creating reusable or modular design assets that fit within the established grid system and get reused throughout a site. These modules not only create design efficiencies, but they also help with usability by repeating recognizable elements that a user can remember.

Modularity can also refer to the necessary design flexibility required in Web design. Some types of Web sites, like news portals, need to accommodate varying lengths and types of content from day to day—even from hour to hour. Therefore, Web design systems for these sites must be flexible to expand and contract as the needs of a site change. This isn't a Web-specific principle; newspapers, magazines, and even corporate identity systems need to have an element of modularity to be effective. What is unique about the Web is the speed with which items in a design need to change (which makes planning ahead an essential part of Web design), the fact that the user can sometimes control the content, and the need for expansion and contraction, making the ultimate outcome unpredictable. Sites that have user-controlled modularity use JavaScript technology to enable users to drag and drop content "blocks" above and below the fold to create their own hierarchy of information.

CHAPTER 6

WEB TYPOGRAPHY

"Typography is the one area in graphic design where there are truly rights and wrongs; there are better-thans and there are randoms."

Alexander W. White
Chairman Emeritus, The Type Directors Club

Why Type Matters

Typography, of all elements of design, can have the greatest effect on the success or failure of a piece of communication. This is because type carries the message, and the craftsmanship of the typography can either enhance or take away from the message. Many designers share a passion for the art of typography and can spend hours kerning letters, adjusting the rag on a column of type, or hanging punctuation. With Web design, however, this level of finite control is difficult, or in some cases not possible at all. But before examining the specific nuances of Web type, it's important to understand a few universal principals of typography.

In historical terms, a font is a complete set of characters that make up a single size, style, and weight of a typeface. The term *typeface* refers to the unique styling applied to a set of glyphs, including an alphabet of letters and ligatures, numerals, and punctuation marks. Due largely to their use in relation to computers, the two terms have evolved to be interchangeable. The term *font* no longer refers to a single size or style, and can even refer to the digital file used by the computer to display typefaces.

It has been said that great typography is invisible, but that's only half the story—typography can also be beautifully expressive and attention-grabbing. In either case, type must carry a message to the user. The two opposing characteristics, which combine to attract a user and convey a message, are called readability and legibility. Both are essential for effective communication.

Readability refers to how well type can attract a reader. Typographic posters, book covers, packaging, logos, and magazine features, for example, must have a readable quality to them in order to get the attention of a reader—a quality that makes a person stop and want to read. Readability can come from size, font usage, composition, color usage, abstraction, or anything that helps type—or, more specifically, the message—stand apart. Effectively readable type expresses meaning through form beyond the content of the words it displays. The FedEx logo is an example of this idea. The bold, geometric shapes of the letterforms imply stability or reliability, while the negative-space arrow between the capital *E* and lowercase *x* implies forward movement and speed—all this with the use of only five letters and two colors.

Legibility, on the other hand, references the ease with which a reader can gather a message, especially when it comes to long stretches of copy. The recognizability of individual characters in a font as well as type size, leading, letter spacing, line length—even color and backgrounds—play a role in how effectively legible type appears. Truly legible type makes it possible for the reader to perceive only content and not be distracted by formatting or decoration.

These two aspects of type play a big part in effective Web typography; however, the level of control a designer has and the methods he or she uses to achieve them can be very different. Readable or expressive typography can be important on the home page to grab the user's attention, define a unique brand characteristic, or alert the reader to a site feature or special offer. Legible type is essential for article or blog text and can make the difference in the success of a site that invites users to return to read long articles or posts.

WebMD.com offers users the ability to change the size of type within an article. This allows the user to control the optimal legibility based on his or her preferences—a concept not possible with conventional print communications. The images below show small, medium, and large type sizes.

Measuring Type

Type and typographic properties such as spacing are commonly measured in em units. An em is a square unit that represents the distance between baselines when type is set without line spacing or leading. An em square is equal to the size of the type; for example, an em space for 12 pixel/point type is a 12-pixel square.

While an em is equal to the type size, the individual characters don't necessarily fit within an em square—they can be larger or smaller. As seen in the diagram below, a Dispatch M fits within a single em unit of 110 points, however the Burgues Script M at the same size is not confined to the em unit.

In Web design—more specifically, CSS styling—type can be defined using em units. Ems are used for relative sizing and for type they're used in the font-size attribute.

Most browsers default to 16-pixel type as a general rule. So if a designer specs type at 75 percent, the size of the type will be 12 pixels. The default can also be altered globally by styling the <body> tag. If in the body tag the font size is set to 62.5 percent, then the default for all type on a site is 10 pixels (16 x .625 = 10). Therefore, the math for defining other sizes become easier: for 15-pixel type the font size would be set to 1.5 em; 24-pixel type would be 2.4 em, etc.

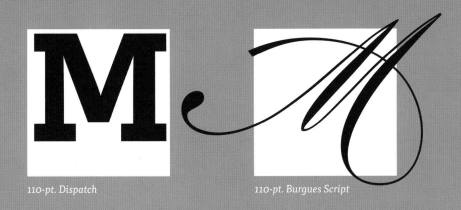

110-pt. Dispatch   110-pt. Burgues Script

The optimal choice for displaying type depends mostly on the **needs of the client** and the **capabilities of the target user.**

While there are limitations to the control a designer has over typographic details on the Web, there are also methods, unique to Web design, of turning over control to the user so he or she may create personalized settings for legibility. Many sites give users the ability to change the size of text, and some sites even give users the option of choosing their own fonts.

Designer Control   User Control

Images of type

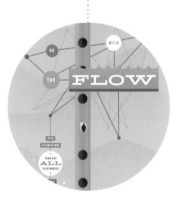

@font-face

Web-safe type

This image of MidtSommerJazz.no shows all three methods of displaying type on the Web— images, Web-safe fonts, and embedded fonts.

Types of Web Type

For years Web designers were constricted to only two options for Web typography— images of type and system fonts (the fonts found universally on devices used to browse the Web). Using images to display type is a static method of rendering type—the type is rendered once by the designer or producer, and that image is distributed throughout the Web to be viewed by the user. Using Web-safe fonts is a means of displaying content as live text, which is rendered by the user's browser. Live text generally offers less control to the designer but more control to the user with which to manipulate aesthetics and/or search the content.

However, that all changed with three important innovations: widespread browser support for the @font-face CSS command; the emergence of font delivery technology; and the development of the Web Open Font Format (WOFF). Now designers have three primary choices when selecting methods of displaying type within a design:

- Images of type
- Web-safe system fonts
- @font-face fonts

Why is this choice so significant? The reason selecting a method with which to display type is so critical to Web design is due to the fact that type delivers content and content drives the success of most Web sites. Content is what users search for. Content is what search engines index and catalog, and search engines can only pull content from live text—images of type are not indexable by search engines. Content, however, must be dressed with some form of style or branding in order to be truly effective for the Web site's owner. Purely displaying content without some sort of visual expressiveness or uniqueness decreases its memorability and therefore decreases its value to the client. The following pages explore examples of each method of displaying type, and details the benefits and drawbacks for each.

Image Type

Images of type offer a Web designer the most control over the typography on a Web page. A designer can freely choose a font from his or her library, adjust the kerning, add filters and effects, etc.—all the things that traditional print designers are used to doing with type. Images of type enable a designer to match branding requirements for a client exactly, or to express a concept precisely as the designer (or client) envisions.

There are a couple of significant drawbacks with this method of displaying type, however. All-image Web sites, where the type is rendered as a jpg, png, or gif image, are extremely limited in their ability to be indexed by search engines, and thus limited in their ability to be found by users. While it's possible to include searchable content within the alt tags—a tag within the image tag that allows the Webmaster to input text describing an image, used mainly for handicapped accessibility—this text does not have a high value with search engines because it can too easily be manipulated to deceive the user.

Served-MCR.com is rich with hand-drawn type and illustrations as well as animations to create a grungy and whimsical look to this site for a ping-pong tournament for creative folks.

The best approach for using images as type on a Web site is to limit the use to particular areas of display type where the images can have the most visual impact. Commonly, designers choose to use images of type for the main navigation of the site; however, this is particularly damaging, as search engines place a high value on linked content. If the main links are images, the links' value cannot be captured by search engines. The bottom line is that images of type are a great way to add personality or brand recognition to a Web site but should be used extremely sparingly in order to maintain the searchability of a site.

The hand-drawn type in this layout for cantilever-chippy.co.uk conveys the sense of a chalk menu board.

Finger-painted letterforms divide up the sections of this page for VintageHope.co.uk. The distinctive look and feel gives the site a memorability that standard headlines may not have.

The identity for the Branding graduate program at the School of Visual Arts is distinctive, creative, and could not be replicated using only Web-safe type. The solution here is to integrate enough of the custom lettering to maintain the recognizability of the brand with Web-safe type for legibility and searchability.

Images of type enable a designer to exactly **match branding requirements** for a client, or **express a concept** precisely as the designer (or client) envisions.

Hand-drawn typography defines this site for Chester Zoo. The kid-like feel of the site reflects the audience the designer and the client were trying to appeal to.

Gnosh.co.uk uses hand-painted type and photography to create a crafted setting in line with the concept of hand-crafted food.

Web-safe Type

With the prevalence of @font-face type available to designers, Web-safe fonts seem to be becoming extinct. Perhaps someday, but for now, Web-safe fonts still offer two distinct and important advantages:

Web-safe fonts were designed specifically for screen use. Fonts like Georgia or Verdana, both designed by type design master Matthew Carter, were created with the intent that they would be used with back-lit conditions and at small sizes. As a result, they have large x-heights, open counter spaces, and wider letterspacing (see diagram) for maximum legibility.

The @font-face command is a series of code and font files that a browser must load in order to render the type. Therefore, they can slow down the load time of a page. Because of this, it is common to use @font-face type for display type and Web-safe fonts for the text or body copy.

Windows	Mac
Arial	Arial, Helvetica
Arial Black	Arial Black, Gadget
Comic Sans MS	Comic Sans MS
Courier New	Courier New, Courier
Georgia	Georgia
Impact	Impact, Charcoal
Lucida Console	Monaco
Lucida Sans Unicode	Lucida Grande
Palatino Linotype	Palatino
Book Antiqua	Georgia
Tahoma	Tahoma
Times New Roman	Times
Trebuchet MS	Trebuchet MS
Verdana	Verdana
Symbol	Symbol
Webdings	Webdings
Wingdings	Zapf Dingbats
MS Sans Serif	Geneva
MS Serif	Georgia

Being able to do **more with less** is an essential skill for a Web designer.

Font Stacks: Designers or coders define Web fonts in the CSS with what is known as a font stack. Font stacks are prioritized lists of fonts, defined in the CSS font-family attribute, that the browser will cycle through until it finds a font that is installed on the user's system. Font stacks list fonts in order of the designer's preference: preferred, alternate, common, generic. Common font stacks include:

font-family = Georgia, [if you don't have that then use] "Times New Roman", [if you don't have that then use] Times, [if you don't have that, please just give me something with a...] serif;

The limitations and unpredictability of font stacks present a challenge to Web designers. Limitations also lead to creative solutions. Doing more with less is an essential skill for a Web designer. The sites pictured here represent a wide visual language using only Web-safe typography.

This stark and stunning layout for decknetwork.net uses only Web-safe type to display the text. The all-caps headline at the top is Georgia, designed by Matthew Carter.

Wordpress.org (above) uses a beautiful mix of Georgia for display type and "sans-serif" for body text.

This all-type solution for the Seed Conference announcement showcases many of the possibilities of CSS type styling. Varying type sizes, colors, and alignments create a clear hierarchy within a unified piece of design.

Jason Santa Maria is considered to be one of Web design's most creative talents. Pictured here are two pages from his site, JasonSantaMaria.com, where he displays his mastery over type, Web type, and imagery integration.

200-POINT GEORGIA

Designed in 1996 by Matthew Carter (hinted for optimal screen viewing by Tom Rickner) specifically for the Web.

200-POINT TIMES ROMAN

Designed in 1931 by Stanley Morison and Victor Lardent (Monotype) for the *Times* newspaper.

atf atf

COUNTERS

The larger counters on Georgia increase legibility

X-HEIGHT

Notice the difference in x-height at the same type size

CAP HEIGHT

Even the height of the capital letters differ at the same point size

BASELINE

The line on which letters sit and the starting point when measuring the x-height and cap height

POINTS & PIXELS

The most common unit of measure when dealing with type is points and picas. There are 72 points in .996 inches and standard screen resolution is 72 pixels per inch (PPI). Therefore, one point is equal to one pixel when referencing elements at screen resolution.

The x-height, represented by the blue line, is the distance between the baseline—where the letters sit—and the top of a lowercase letter. It's clear to see that Georgia, designed by Matthew Carter specifically for the Web, has a higher x-height than Times Roman at the same size. A counter is the "hole" created in letters like a lowercase a. In Georgia, the counters are larger and more open. These characteristics combine to make Georgia more legible that other serif typefaces when viewed on screen.

AListApart.com, uses a beautiful combination of Web-safe type (Georgia for the body text) and @font-face (Franklin Gothic for the display type). This cohesive, type-driven layout has defined the A List Apart brand for many years.

Portico · *front page* | Home · *sweet home* | Archive · *and search* | Contact · *and email* | Subscribe · *via rss*

ALPHA AESTHETICA

1. OPTIMIZATION VS. HARDWARE PROCUREMENT
How buying hardware is often the cheapest way to solve computational complexity.

2. NEW FEATURES OF C# 4.0 *by Mads Torgersen*
True dynamic typing and type safe co- & contra-variance

3. N-CORE PERFORMANCE TO PLATEAU *by R Murphy*
Could off-die memory latency one day force fundamental changes to architectures?

· Promo ·

hire
ME
TYPESETTING
GRAPHIC / .NET WIN & WEB
DESIGN / DEVELOPMENT

· Preface ·

OH, HELLO. HERE LIE A
COLLECTION OF ARTICLES,
NARRATIVES AND
PONDERINGS OF COMPUTERY
THINGS; FINELY BLENDED
WITH MY PORTFOLIO
BESTOWING WORKS AND
EXPERIMENTS IN U.I. DESIGN,
INFOGRAPHICS, AND
SOFTWARE DEVELOPMENT.
BON APPÉTIT.

· Calendar ·

MAY 2010

MO	TU	WE	TH	FR	SA	SU
					1	2
3	4	5	6	7	8	9
10	11	12	13	14	15	16
17	18	19	20	21	22	23
24	25	26	27	28	29	30
31						

· Categories ·

	POSTS	RSS
CYNOSURA	0	RSS
GENERAL	0	RSS
GRAPHIC DESIGN	4	RSS
PROGRAMMING	5	RSS
WWW TECH	3	RSS

*Raymond S. Glover
Cynosura*

THE ARCHIVES

10 ENTRIES SPANNING 1 YEAR, 2 MONTHS, 1 WEEK,
1 DAY AND 11 HOURS

Enter search term

SEARCH

☐ INCLUDE COMMENTS IN SEARCH

CATEGORY	RSS
1. Cynosura	subscribe
2. General	subscribe
3. Graphic Design	subscribe
4. Programming	subscribe
5. WWW Tech	subscribe

1. Cynosura

DATE	TITLE	COMMENTS	RATING
	Total	0	NONE

2. General

DATE	TITLE	COMMENTS	RATING
	Total	0	NONE

3. Graphic Design

DATE	TITLE	COMMENTS	RATING
2009-09-19	RENDERING LONDON	7	4
2009-03-01	PIXELS IN VECTORS	23	4.5
2009-01-31	GROWTH RATES	10	5
2008-12-29	DICTIONARY UI MOCKUPS	3	4.6
	Total	43	4.5

4. Programming

DATE	TITLE	COMMENTS	RATING
2010-03-06	JSON PRETTY PRINTER	0	NONE
2009-03-02	SOCKETS AND C#	15	4
2009-01-27	THE TIMESPAN ARTICULATOR	5	5
2008-12-28	THE COWON S9, REVERSE ENGINEERED	14	4.5
2008-12-26	A LINE MAPPING STREAMREADER	3	NONE
	Total	37	4.5

5. WWW Tech

DATE	TITLE	COMMENTS	RATING
2009-09-19	RENDERING LONDON	7	4
2008-12-30	THE SEMANTIC WEB	17	4.8
	Total	24	4.4

Overview

10 posts by 2 author(s)
97 comments by 86 reader(s)
39 raters averaging 4.6

Weblog.Cynosura.eu seamlessly mixes images of type with Web-safe type— with the majority shown here being Web safe. The centered layout and delicate line work give the site a classic beauty.

Portico · *front page* | Home · *sweet home* | Archive · *and search* | Contact · *and email* | Subscribe · *via rss*

ALPHA AESTHETICA

LAT

1. OPTIMIZATION VS. HARDWARE PROCUREMENT
How buying hardware is often the cheapest way to solve computational complexity.

2. NEW FEATURES OF C# 4.0 *by Mads Torgersen*
True dynamic typing and type safe co- & contra-variance

3. N-CORE PERFORMANCE TO PLATEAU *by R Murphy*
Could off-die memory latency one day force fundamental changes to architectures?

· Promo ·

hire
ME
TYPESETTING
GRAPHIC / .NET WIN & WEB
DESIGN / DEVELOPMENT

· Preface ·

OH, HELLO. HERE LIE A
COLLECTION OF ARTICLES,
NARRATIVES AND
PONDERINGS OF COMPUTERY
THINGS; FINELY BLENDED
WITH MY PORTFOLIO
BESTOWING WORKS AND
EXPERIMENTS IN U.I. DESIGN,
INFOGRAPHICS, AND
SOFTWARE DEVELOPMENT.
BON APPÉTIT.

JSON

Does what is says on t
year ago after a failed
light and simple JS r

· Calendar ·

· Categories ·

InkAndSpindle.com, seen on this page, uses the Google Font Muli designed by Vernon Adams. The minimalist font can be used for both headlines and body text as seen here.

@Font-face Type

In truth, the @font-face command existed in CSS2 and dates back to 1998, but there is a problem with it when used by itself. @font-face uses font files located on a server to display a typeface in a browser exactly the same way images appear on a server and are displayed on a page. Therefore, with very little hacking ability, any user of a Web page would have the ability to download the fonts used on any given Web page. This was a big problem for font designers and the foundries that represent them. Fonts represent valuable intellectual property, and distributing them freely through the Web significantly devalues them.

From this need came a plethora of font-delivery systems. Font-delivery systems like Fontdeck, typekit, WebType, TypeCloud, and Google Fonts, among many others, use proprietary code to deliver fonts to a user's browser without ever revealing the font files to the user. Now, designers can license and use fonts from a seemingly limitless library. And type designers and foundries can protect their intellectual property.

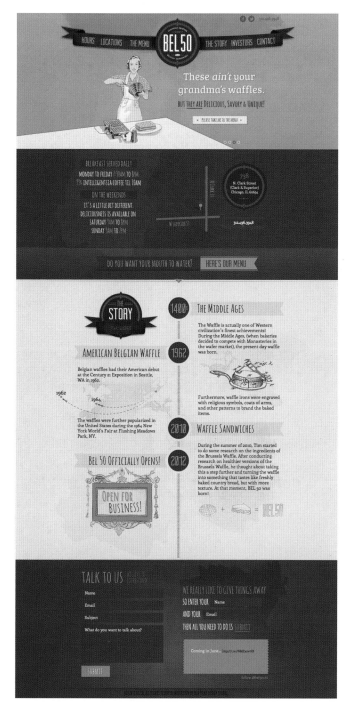

This makes the need for using Web-safe system fonts less critical, but there are still very good reasons to rely on Web-safe fonts: most Web-safe fonts, like Georgia or Verdana, were designed specifically for screen use; they have design characteristics that make them more legible when viewed at small sizes on a screen; and the @font-face command, like imagery, can add load times to a page.

Grumpy wizards make toxic brew for the evil Queen and Jack.

Normal 400

Grumpy wizards make toxic brew for the

Bold 700

Grumpy wizards make toxic brew for th

One morning, when Gregor Samsa woke from troubled dreams, he found himself transformed in his bed into a horrible vermin. He lay on his armour-like back, and if he lifted his head a little he could see his brown belly, slightly domed and divided by arches into stiff sections. The bedding was hardly able to cover it and seemed ready to slide off any moment. His many legs, pitifully thin compared with the size of the rest of him, waved about helplessly as he looked.

Bel50.com uses the Google Font Enriqueta slab serif for the body text, a font that was created by combining robust and strong serifs from the Egyptian style with softer tones from Roman typefaces.

Fonts represent **valuable intellectual property** and @font-face leaves some question as to the end user's ability to reuse the font without paying for it.

Font styling is one of the most exciting and complicated areas of Web typography. However, it is not the only area of focus for a designer. Web typography, like all forms of typographic expression, needs to illustrate a clear sense of hierarchy through the use of scale, color, and typeface. The examples shown here aren't meant only to dazzle with their typefaces, but to use the typefaces to convey a clear message.

KCCreepFest.com has a hand-drawn feel thanks to the Google Font Homemade Apple. The use of this font gives the site a feel of handwriting with the searchability of native type.

Grumpy wizards make toxic brew for the evil Queen and Jack.

Normal 400

Grumpy wizards make toxic brew

One morning, when Gregor Samsa woke from troubled dreams, he found himself transformed in his bed into a horrible vermin. He lay on his armour-like back, and if he lifted his head a little he could see his brown belly, slightly domed and divided by arches into stiff sections. The bedding was hardly able to cover it and seemed ready to slide off any moment. His many legs, pitifully thin compared with the size of the rest of him, waved about helplessly as he looked.

| FEATURE

100 Years Of Olympic Logos: A Depressing History Of Design Crimes

There's some beautiful graphic design on exhibit in these 45 Olympic Games logos, but most of them make you go WTF.

READ MORE ›

41 NOTES   1.1K TWEET   3.0K LIKE

| FEATURE

100 Years Of Olympic Logos: A Depressing History Of Design Crimes

There's some beautiful graphic design on exhibit in these 45 Olympic Games logos, but most of them make you go WTF.

READ MORE ›

41 NOTES   1.1K TWEET   3.0K LIKE

Between
ECONOMICS AND LIFE
MARKETPLACE®
LISTEN NOW

Co.Design
business + innovation + design

Editor Suzanne LaBarre

Subscribe to Newsletters

ENTER YOUR EMAIL:
submit

FastCoDesign.com uses a mix of MuseoSans, a sans serif text font, and FCZizouSlab, a custom display font for headlines. The combination creates a nice contrast between display and text type.

Co.Design
business + innovation + design
Editor Suzanne
Sub

A Designer Teach Pirates To Knock Off His Luxury

...nd in doing so, prove that you can never counterfeit quality.

READ MORE ›

45 NOTES   712 TWEET   9.3K LIKE

INFOGRAPHIC OF THE DAY

Can This Clever Statistical Model Predict Olympic Medal Winners?

EDITOR'S PICKS

100 Years Of Olympic Logos: A Depressing History Of Design Crimes

Subscribe to Newsletters

ENTER YOUR EMAIL:
submit

Comic Book Heroes Get A Gorgeous Native American Makeover

Batman, Superman, and Spider-Man look truly stunning following a traditional, Pacific Northwest makeover.

READ MORE ›

10 NOTES   566 TWEET   15.3K LIKE

INFOGRAPHIC OF THE DAY

Can This Clever Statistical Model Predict Olympic Medal Winners?

EDITOR'S PICKS

100 Years Of Olympic Logos: A Depressing History Of Design Crimes

ENTER YOUR EMAIL:
submit

INFOGRAPHIC OF THE DAY

Infographics Lie. Here's How To Spot The B.S.

Infographics are all over the place nowadays. How do you know which ones to trust? Follow these three easy steps to save yourself from getting duped.

READ MORE ›

6 NOTES   1.0K TWEET   2.0K LIKE

London SE is a little guide to finding the best spots in London's unsung south east corner.

Hunhead Cemetery

LONDON SE

This site, London-se.com, uses a complex mix of serif, sans serif, condensed, and regular type to create a beautiful typographically-driven layout. The fonts used are Calofax, Elena, and Publico Headline.

Weights and Styles

AaBbCcDdEeFfGgHhIiJjKkLlMmNnOoPpQqRrSsTtUuVv
Elena Web Basic Regular

AaBbCcDdEeFfGgHhIiJjKkLlMmNnOoPpQqRrSsTtUuVvWwXx
Elena Web Basic Regular Italic

AaBbCcDdEeFfGgHhIiJjKkLlMmNnOoPpQqRrSsTtU
Elena Web Basic Bold

AaBbCcDdEeFfGgHhIiJjKkLlMmNnOoPpQqRrSsTtUuVv
Elena Web Basic Bold Italic

Weights and Styles

AaBbCcDdEeFfGgHhIiJj KkLlMmNnOoPpQqRrSsTtU
Calofax Thin Roman and Italic

AaBbCcDdEeFfGgHhIiJj KkLlMmNnOoPpQqRrSsTtU
Calofax Light Roman and Italic

AaBbCcDdEeFfGgHhIiJj KkLlMmNnOoPpQqRrSsTtU
Calofax Regular Roman and Italic

AaBbCcDdEeFfGgHhIiJj KkLlMmNnOoPpQqRrSsT
Calofax Medium Roman and Italic

Favourite Spots

Just Added

Coffee Shop
ST. DAVID COFFEE HOUSE
FOREST HILL

Pub
**THE TELEGRAPH
(AT THE EARL OF DERBY)**
TELEGRAPH HILL

Wine Bar
MR. LAWRENCE
BROCKLEY

Bar
PECKHAM PELICAN
PECKHAM

Fishmonger
F.C. SOPER
NUNHEAD

ALL OF OUR FAVOURITE SPOTS

PECKHAM   NEW CROSS   BLAC

LONDON SE MAP   BROCKLEY   LEWISHAM

HERNE HILL   DULWICH

Elsewhere
🅕 🅣 ◉

Enter your email to receive our newsletter

SUBMIT

Ongoing Exhibitions

Until 23 February 2014

**Astronomy Photographer
of the Year**

Royal Observatory

Details on rmg.co.uk

Until 23 February 2014

**Uri Aran: Five Minute
Before**

South London Gallery

southlondongallery.org

Until 16 February 2014

Life on the Road

**London College of
Communication**

Details on ual.com

Until 9 March 2014

**Hello My Name is Paul
Smith**

The Design Museum

Details on designmuseum.org

Until 27 April 2014

**Martin Creed: What's the
Point of It?**

Hayward Gallery

southbankcentre.co.uk

ALL ONGOING EXHIBITIONS

© London SE 2013

🅕 Like ⟨ 88 ⟩
🅣 Follow @London_SE

Who and what are we?

London SE is from Brendan Evans and Sophie Latham, a web designer and school teacher — currently somewhere in Peckham or Brockley.

Contact us

Know of a place that deserves mention? Found some wrong or outdated info? Want to say hi? Email us at hello@london-se.com or send us a tweet or two.

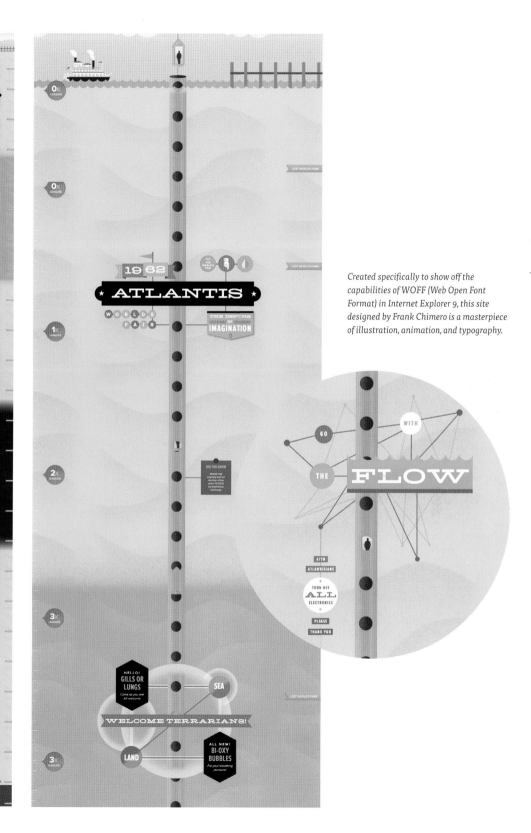

Created specifically to show off the
capabilities of WOFF (Web Open Font
Format) in Internet Explorer 9, this site
designed by Frank Chimero is a masterpiece
of illustration, animation, and typography.

The openface design of the type on Fixate.it matches the line illustrations used throughout the site. Creating unity between type and image.

IN CULP
Culpa qu

QUI OFFICIA DES
Officia deserunt m

DESERUNT MOLLIT ANIM
Mollit anim id est laborum. I.

ANIM ID EST LA
Id est laborum. Lo

EST LABORUM. LOREM I
Laborum. Lorem ipsum dol
or sit amet, consectetur adi

LOREM IPSUM DOLOR SIT AMET.
ipsum dolor sit amet, consectetur ad
ipiscing elit, sed do eiusmod tempor

Grumpy wizards make toxic brew for the evil Queen and Jack.

Grumpy wizards make toxic brew for th

We are a web, illustration, & design agency

We create cutting-edge designs, websites, & web applications for companies & individuals who love the limelight.

We're a driven company with a simple goal – to make your business stand head and shoulders above the rest. We combine engaging design with state-of-the-art development, whilst always keeping the client's needs at the heart of every creative idea we have. We make it our duty to ensure the success of your business – after all – if you do well, a little of the light shines on us.

fixate
web & design

re a web, tration, & gn agency

cutting-edge designs, websites, & web applications for & individuals who love the limelight.

n company with a simple goal – to make your business stand head and shoulders above the combine engaging design with state-of-the-art development, whilst always keeping the client's needs heart of every creative idea we have. We make it our duty to ensure the success of your business – all – if you do well, a little of the light shines on us.

In an increasingly digital world, a strong online presence is imperative.

We use our muscles to build intuitive and attractive websites that connect you with your customers. We specialise in thoughtful design that will enhance your brand and set you apart from the clamour of your competitors. All of our projects are executed at the highest standard, and we endeavour to remain ahead of the curve by keeping up to date with new and advanced technologies.

Publicity

We're thrilled at the positive response our site has received from people around the world! We've even been featured on some respected design and development sites and wanted to share a few with you.

- Awwwards Site Of The Day – 1 Dec 2013
- The Best Designs
- Web Design Ledger
- Zurb Responsive Website Gallery

The designer of ChrisWilhiteDesign.com used bold condensed sans serif type contrasing with serif type to create a definite visual statement that is as distinctive as the products being shown on the site.

Display type on wineshop.hunters.co.nz is replaced using Cufón. Different than @font-face, JavaScript applications like Cufón use SVG graphics to display searchable type without using the font files.

HUNTER'S
MARLBOROUGH

Show the   Show all

White   Red   Sparkling

Order by   Price   Vintage

← Back to Hunters.co.nz

09 Breidecker

Bottle	Case
$17.90	$135.60
☐ QTY	☐ QTY

Details   Add to cart

08 Chardonnay

Bottle	Case
$19.90	$169.80
☐ QTY	☐ QTY

Details   Add to cart

09 Gewurztraminer

Bottle	Case
$22.90	$249.60
☐ QTY	☐ QTY

Details   Add to cart

08 Kaho Roa

Bottle	Case
$23.90	$204.00
☐ QTY	☐ QTY

Details   Add to cart

08 MiruMiru

Bottle	Case
$22.50	$135.00
☐ QTY	☐ QTY

Details   Add to cart

08 Pinot Noir

Bottle	Case
$26.90	$226.80
☐ QTY	☐ QTY

Details   Add to cart

09 Riesling

Bottle	Case
$19.90	$169.80
☐ QTY	☐ QTY

Details   Add to cart

09 Rosé

Bottle	Case
$15.00	$135.60
☐ QTY	☐ QTY

Details   Add to cart

09 Sauvignon Blanc

Bottle	Case
$19.90	$169.80
☐ QTY	☐ QTY

Details   Add to cart

07 Sauvignon Blanc

Bottle	Case
$19.90	$169.80
☐ QTY	☐ QTY

Details   Add to cart

08 The Chase

Bottle	Case
$15.00	$153.90
☐ QTY	☐ QTY

Details   Add to cart

THE WINE STORE

About Hunters

Jane Hunter has been described by the London Sunday Times as "the star of New Zealand wine".

In 1983 Jane and her late husband Ernie founded their first fledgling winery in the picturesque Wairau Valley, Marlborough. Since then Hunter's have won more than 125 gold medals at national and international wine competitions, including the Marquis de Goulaine Trophy for Best Sauvignon Blanc in the World.

As a fitting tribute, exactly 25 years after starting Hunter's Wines, Jane Hunter was appointed a Companion of the New Zealand Order of Merit for services to viticulture.

Jane Hunter

Wine Orders

All prices are in New Zealand Dollars and include GST.

You must be 18 years or older to order.

We reserve the right to restrict sales should orders exceed supply.

We aim to please. If you're not 100% happy, please return your purchase for a complete refund.

Delivery

Delivery is available within New Zealand only and may take up to two weeks.

All orders must be a multiple of 6.

For international enquiries please refer to our local **agents**.

Contact Us

Hunter's Wines Ltd.
Rapaura Road, Blenheim
PO Box 5094, Springlands 7241.
Telephone +64 3 572-8489
NZ Freephone 0800 486 847

Email Us

Not all @font-face Web typography needs to be big, bold, and in your face. This example, TheRivetPress.com, uses beautifully crafted details to create a distinctive and elegant look. The site uses Brandon Grotesque along with Web-safe Georgia.

— presents —

THE RIVET PRESS

A HIUT DENIM PRODUCTION

ALL ARTICLES
View all The Rivet Press articles in one uninterrupted flow of consciousness.

SCRAPBOOK CHRONICLES
A carefully curated selection from the web that caught our eye and inspired us.

WORKSHOP WISDOM
Andrew Paynter visits maker's workshops to document the creative process.

HISTORY TAG TALES
Witness the lives and adventures of Hiut jeans through the eyes of their wearers.

THE FACTORY
News, media and all the latest behind the scenes from our small denim factory.

MAKERS & MAVERICKS
Our list of 100 movers and shakers that made a real change in 2013.

A COLLECTION OF WORDS
Essays, articles and articulate musings from Hiut Co-Founder, David Hieatt.

INSPIRATION
An all visual tumble of hand collected images and optical stimulation.

A Week In Instagram / No. 007

THE FACTORY

REFINE

01
If you run a company make sure it doesn't end up running you. You will have more ideas when you learn to switch off.

Search our content for Artisans. We celebrate the skilled craftsmen and the makers.

02
Sunshine trying to break on through.

Search our content for Denim. Whether Hiut Denim or others, it will all be here.

Search our content for Design. From architecture to stationary, everything has a designer.

03
Paul has brought in his old jeans to practice on. #freerepairsforlife #rawdenim

Search our content for Farm. We farm ideas but we still get our hands & our Hiuts dirty.

Search our content for Food. A healthy mind requires a healthy appetite.

04
Storm blowing. Candles lit. Power cuts expected. #wildwest #cardiganbay

Search our content for Inspiration. Click the flame and light that fire.

Search our content for Music. Discover what tunes keep our Grandmasters sewing.

05
Calm. #notsowildwest

Search our content for Environment. Wherever you live, this is vital.

06
Good food plus good design equals good book.

Search our content for Tech. The best and the brightest from the technological world.

SHARE

NEWER | HOME | OLDER

ABOUT
The Rivet Press is a Hiut Denim production, an online home for the Hiut community to grow, interact and get inspired.

In our factory we make jeans and we make them well. Online, we stitch ideas, unbutton dreams and press out the wrinkles. To read Hiut's story, click here.

MAKERS & MAVERICKS
At the end of 2013, the Hiut team got together to compile a list of the one hundred biggest influencers of the year. The people that made a difference, made a change, that went against the grain in favour of innovation and progress.

To see the full list, click here.

THE YEARBOOK

CONTACT
Email: stephanie@therivetpress.com

Instagram: @hiutdenim
Twitter: @hiutdenim
Google+: Follow
Facebook: HiutDenimCo

Sign up to the Newsletter

SITE BY THE PRINTER'S SON & POSITIVELY MELANCHOLY FOR HIUT DENIM

OPTIMIZE

CHAPTER 7

SEARCH ENGINE OPTIMIZATION

Clients are always looking for the maximum financial return possible on their Web project investment. Return on investment (ROI) is critical because developing a Web site can be quite expensive, and organizations need to show value for the money they invest in a Web project. While design plays an enormous role in building a strong brand, and well thought-out usability gives customers a great experience, neither matters if the target audience cannot find a site. Attracting the maximum possible number of site visitors is essential for the success of a site—and, in turn, the success of the company that owns the site. Simply put, getting found is everything to a business.

Getting Discovered: Browsing & Searching

There are three primary ways a user finds a specific site: by typing an address (URL) directly into the browser address bar; by browsing and following links or advertisements from one site to another; or by searching a topic in a search engine such as Google. While there's some debate over this topic, most research shows that well over half of Internet users start by searching a topic using a search engine. This chapter explores the considerations one must make while planning, designing, coding, and promoting a site so search engines can find and index it.

Just like with Web design and Web usability, search engine optimization (SEO) is continually evolving based on trends and market factors. It would be difficult to codify specific techniques in a book whose usefulness is intended to last beyond the publication date. Therefore, this chapter focuses on the conceptual foundation of SEO—the basic principles that form the core of various trends. The exact techniques for a specific market or site can easily be found, ironically, by searching the Web for SEO. Understanding why SEO is important, and the basic principles that influence effective results, helps a designer approach the planning and creation of a site with the correct mindset.

Types of Search Engines

There are two types of search engines:

Crawler based, like Bing.com and Google.com, which find sites using spiders to crawl the Web and index content. A spider is a software tool that seeks out heavily trafficked servers for popular sites. Spiders are programmed to follow every link within a site while indexing the words it finds on each page. Crawler-based search engines gather information about a site and rank that site based on a series of on-site and external factors that will be explored in this chapter.

Directories, such as dmoz.org, rely on volunteer editors to evaluate sites for a specific topic and determine whether they should be listed in the directory. While these types of directories provide highly relevant sites, the process of selecting sites can be slow, which can result in some newer sites not appearing in the directory. Directory sites, however, can provide significant SEO value to a site that is listed with them. The inbound links (IBL) from popular directories to a site help to dramatically raise that site's ranking with crawler-based search engines.

For the sake of clarity in this chapter, it is important to define a couple of terms: a browser is an application installed on the user's computer and is used to browse and display Web pages. Some popular browsers are Internet Explorer, Safari, and Firefox. A search engine is a Web site or Web utility that catalogs sites, through various means,

Top Crawler-Based Search Engines

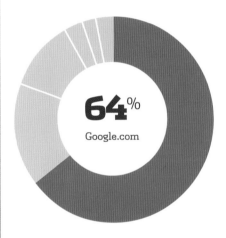

Google	64%
Yahoo!	16%
Bing	11%
AOL Search	3%
Ask	2%
Other	3%

Source: Nielsen MegaView Search

Just like with Web design and Web usability, search engine optimization (SEO) techniques are **continually evolving** based on trends and market factors.

Google™

bing™

YAHOO!

Google, Yahoo!, and Bing are the three most widely used crawler-based search engines on the Internet.

and presents the user with a list of sites that are relevant to the user's search. Some popular search engines are Google, Yahoo! and Bing. A browser requires the user to know the exact domain name or URL of a site, beginning with www. and ending with .com, .org, etc., while a search engine requires only that a user have a topic he or she would like to find out more about.

The goal of any search engine is to sort through the millions of Web sites on the Internet and deliver the most popular and relevant sites to a user based on a search term or phrase. The goal of a Webmaster is to stand out from the millions of sites and get his or her site listed however possible. It's an ever-evolving cat-and-mouse game where the rules change over time.

Early search engines relied mostly on site content when developing their rankings. A spider would simply read the text and the markup (the tags and code unseen by the user) to determine the content type and quality of a page. Some of these hidden bits of markup code include meta keywords, which can be listed in the <head> tag of the HTML and are intended to be the key terms and phrases used in the content of the page; the meta description, which is also found in the <head> tag and briefly describes the content of a page; and alt text (alternative text), which is a written description of a photo, for example, that can be translated to speech for vision-impaired users.

One issue with this method of cataloging is that these unseen tags can be filled with irrelevant terms that are nevertheless designed to yield high traffic. Say, for example, a Webmaster launched a site for a brand-new widget. It's unlikely that anyone

would be searching for this widget, so he might load the meta tags with terms related to cars—even though his widget has nothing to do with cars—because he knows millions of people search for terms related to cars every day. He may even put some white text talking about cars on his home page on a white background—white on white wouldn't be seen by the user but would be read as content by the spider. Within time, this widget site would begin appearing on searches for "cars," however, when a user clicked on the link looking for car information, he or she would be disappointed to see that this site had no actual content related to cars—only widgets. This is called spamdexing or Black Hat SEO.

Additionally, as the Internet evolved through the 1990s and into the 2000s, so did the types of content on Web sites. So-called "rich media," such as Flash, audio, and video content, cannot be indexed by search engines using typical methods. Since spiders cannot listen to, watch, or interact with content, sites that employ rich content were not ranking.

Search engines quickly caught on and began adjusting their methods of ranking sites to reduce spam, detect Black Hat tactics, and increase the ranking of sites that employed rich media like video. While some search engines continue to employ a site's meta description as the brief blurb under the link on a search results page, meta descriptions are not weighted heavily when ranking the site. Nor are meta keywords, alt tags, or other elements not seen by the end user, because of the ease with which they can be manipulated. Instead, search engines now use a combination of a site's popularity, in addition to its content, to determine their rank for the site. To do this, search engines not only look at onsite elements like title tags—the text that appears in the top of the browser window—but also offsite factors like the domain name's age and links from other sites. In fact, offsite factors have a greater effect on a site's rank than do on-site factors. By effectively understanding which sites are the most popular in relation to specific search terms, search engines can reasonably ensure that the content is relevant to users who search those terms.

Elements and Weight of Google Ranking

1. Trust in the Host Domain

2. Link Popularity

3. Anchor Text of External Links

4. On-Page Keyword Usage

5. Traffic and Click-Through Rate

6. Social Graph Metrics

7. Registration and Host Data

Source: http://www.seomoz.org/article/search-ranking-facto

The Wild West

As search engines get more sophisticated in their methods of evaluating sites, so too, do the individuals who intend to manipulate the results. A high search ranking can have a significant monetary value for an organization or an individual. As a result, the competition to reach the top with high-volume terms can get fierce. When money is involved, there's usually someone trying to cheat the system.

Honest, content-based methods of SEO, like those discussed in this chapter, are called White Hat *techniques—named for the good guys who always wore white in the Wild West movies. Conversely, Black Hat SEO tactics are deceitful and manipulative. Those who practice Black Hat SEO are generally looking for traffic volume for its own sake—not to entertain, inform, or in any way provide value to the user.*

Search engines retain the right to punish sites that practice Black Hat or deceitful tactics (knowingly or unknowingly) by removing them from their lists.

It's essential to select keywords based on the **customer's point of view**—not necessarily the client's internal vernacular.

Keywords

Before one can begin the process of implementing either on-site or external SEO techniques, one must first determine the best keywords for the site. Keywords are the specific terms that relate directly to the content of a site that people might use in their search. It's essential to select these terms based on the customer's point of view—not necessarily the client's point of view. Very often, clients speak of themselves using internal language—like product names or industry terms—that don't reflect how users search for information. It's important to understand how a user would define a client's business and use terms that fit that idea.

Users generally search for the solution to a problem they're experiencing: "What is [blank]?" "I need a [blank]," or "Where is [blank]?" Therefore, an effective strategy for developing a list of keywords is to position them as the answer to a question. These might be single words, but two-, three-, and even four-word phrases can be used. Identifying these words and phrases can involve a few methods.

Keyword tools such as the Google Keyword Tool, as well as third-party pay services, like WordTraker, help identify terms. These services are connected to a database of popular search terms and can cross-reference a specific term with other, synonymous terms that may have also been used to find sites related to the same topic. They can also provide information on the volume, popularity, and competition of terms as well.

Site-indexing tools crawl a site and provide a list of the current keyword mix. This is a good place to start implementing an SEO strategy on an existing site.

(Opposite) This is a screenshot from the Google Keyword Tool. Searching the phrase "Web design books" produces the list of additional keyword ideas seen here. The list is helpful for determining the right balance of competition and monthly user searches— too much competition makes a word hard to target, yet too few monthly searches make a word less than valuable.

Old-fashioned brainstorming, or role-playing—"If I were a user, what would I search?"—can produce a valuable list of terms that can act as a starting point before using a keyword tool.

When developing a list of key terms or phrases, it's important to think of broad enough terms, so there's an adequate amount of search volume, but not so broad that there are so many results that competing for the top spot would be impossible. For example, imagine a site that sells golf shirts patterned after retro shirts from the 1950s. Simply using the term *golf* would be problematic, since there are roughly 416 million search results for the term *golf*—everything from golf clinics and clubs to golf vacations and books. However, the phrase *1950s golf shirts* is too specific and may not yield the search volume that the client is looking for. Therefore, phrases like *classic golf shirts* or *buy retro shirts* might produce the right volume of qualified traffic with a reasonable ability to rank highly.

Keywords or phrases should not only accurately and specifically describe the content on a site; they should also be tailored to promoting conversion—a topic that's explored further in the next chapter. Most sites have a specific action they would like a user to take: sign up, buy, log in, etc. For these sites, it's not enough to simply be found—it's important to drive visitors who are looking to take action, so the keywords chosen for the site can include verbs like buy, as in the previous example, to promote high-value traffic—not just high volume.

Keyword lists should be kept at a manageable length—25 to 75 words, depending on the size and type of site. A list that's too long can dilute the effectiveness of each individual keyword. Consistency and repetition is important for SEO, and a long list of words cuts down on the writer's ability to repeat terms. Although, it should be noted, some search engines may flag as spam a repetition of the exact same phrase numerous times, and this can be detrimental to a site's ranking. The terms that people use to search, and the concepts, ideas, and words used on a site, evolve constantly—and therefore so should the list of SEO keywords. The list should be revisited frequently enough to be sure all of the terms are current and connected to the user.

Keyword	Competition	Global Monthly Searches	Local Monthly Searches	Local Search Trends
web design books		9,900	4,400	
web page design templates		110,000	74,000	
web page design templates		74,000	40,500	
web page design		165,000	110,000	
web page design tutorial		14,800	6,600	
web page design software		90,500	60,500	
flash web page design		368,000	165,000	
web page design tools		33,100	18,100	
web design courses		49,500	18,100	
learn web design		9,900	6,600	
professional web page design		18,100	12,100	
web design tools		14,800	8,100	
sample web page design		12,100	6,600	
web graphic design		60,500	49,500	
web page design jobs		18,100	14,800	
web page design layout		9,900	4,400	
freelance web designer		49,500	14,800	
learn web page design		4,400	3,600	
web page design ideas		2,900	1,900	
cool web page design		8,100	6,600	
web design studio		27,100	6,600	
web page design prices		6,600	4,400	
web design awards		18,100	9,900	
web design jobs		33,100	14,800	
web design company		201,000	90,500	
top web design		90,500	49,500	
flash web design		90,500	49,500	
web page design tips		3,600	1,600	
award winning web design		4,400	2,900	
web page design examples		12,100	6,600	
web page designer career		880	720	
custom web page design		22,200	14,800	
web design tutorial		27,100	9,900	
web design ideas		8,100	5,400	
personal web page design		49,500	40,500	
web design and development		90,500	40,500	
web page design cost		12,100	9,900	
web design software		165,000	74,000	
best web design		74,000	40,500	
good web design		12,100	6,600	
professional web design		60,500	33,100	
web design magazine		5,400	2,400	
great web design		5,400	2,900	
web design tips		12,100	5,400	
good web design examples		14,800	8,100	
artistic web design		720	590	
creative web design		22,200	8,100	
web design prices		27,100	14,800	
web design london		33,100	8,100	
web design services		110,000	60,500	

Go to page: 1 Show rows: 50 1 - 50 of 800

Designing for Spiders

Once a keyword list has been developed, it's time to begin employing those keywords on the site in ways that provide the most value for search engines. It's important to note that SEO factors shift in their overall importance, and no one factor will have a significant impact. It's the combination of these ideas and the management of them over time that creates an effective SEO strategy.

When designing for SEO, it's important to remember the two most basic things about how a search engine ranks pages:

- Is this page what it claims to be?
- How popular is this page?

The former is done by highlighting—visually and technically—specific key phrases that describe the page. The latter is done by linking to the page, as we will discuss later in this chapter.

While the majority of SEO techniques center around developing content and establishing relationships with like-minded sites, designers can have an impact on the SEO value of a site. Designing for SEO means using Web-specific design methods, especially when it comes to displaying content, that yield visually interesting and dynamic results that search engines can index. This involves planning for an appropriate mix of graphics, animation, and content. Often, sites go too far toward one end of the spectrum or the other; too much of an SEO focus and a page can look generic or under-designed, while too much of a design focus, such as overuse of Flash or graphics for key text items, can result in poor search engine ranking. However, having an effectively optimized site doesn't mean it can't be designed well, and vice versa. It's simply a matter of employing the correct techniques.

The AIGA NY site employs many SEO best practices both seen and unseen. The site architecture is clear for easy crawling by spiders; links and headlines are filled with valuable keywords; and the source code is concisely written.

Designing for SEO means using **Web-specific design methods**, especially when it comes to displaying content, that yield visually interesting and dynamic results that search engines can index.

In previous chapters, this book explored the pros and cons of various means of displaying type—or, more accurately, content. Using methods to display "live" text (as opposed to images of text) is important, but the concept of designing for SEO goes beyond just using Web-safe type. The designer's arrangement of content is critical to effective SEO. Important, keyword-rich content should be displayed above the fold—the higher the better. The content should be broken up with headings and subheads, not only for scannability, but for SEO as well. Keyword-rich headings and subheadings should be styled using the "H" tags: <H1>, <H2>, <H3>, etc. The content in these tags is given greater weight by spiders since it is likely to contain information about the key ideas on the page.

Having keywords above the fold for the user to see is important, but equally—if not more—important is having keywords appear as high as possible in the HTML code for the spiders to find. To do this, pages should be built using CSS and <div> tags rather than tables. Using tables, an older method of building page structures with rows and columns, results in longer code that can push down content in the markup. The CSS styling should be imported from an exterior CSS style sheet to avoid having long stretches of CSS code in the <head> tag of a page. The same is true for JavaScript functions, or anything that can unnecessarily lengthen the markup.

Images can play a role in SEO as well. Since images saved by a designer are the exact same images that get downloaded by the user for display in a browser, the file names are important. Keyword-rich file names can help SEO—widget.jpg instead of img_123.jpg, for example.

Arranging content and creating assets in a way that's both user-friendly and spider-friendly is a unique challenge for a Web designer. However, a designer can only have so much influence on the overall SEO strategy. An all-encompassing SEO strategy involves collaboration among a designer, a copywriter, the development team, the client, and even a media planner. What follows are other SEO factors that designers should be aware of, but which often are the responsibility of others on the team.

To the right are excerpts from the code for the Web page seen on the far right, MillerWhiteSchool.org. Only some of the important SEO features are displayed here, including:

- Title tag, *which appears as part of the browser window above. It contains valuable keywords that users might search to find a school.*

- The meta description *is used by Google and other search engines to describe a site.*

- The meta keywords *are no longer heavily weighted by search engines but should be included nonetheless.*

- The navigation *is text based and filled with keywords.*

- The <H1> tag *is actually the logo on the page. The text is indented off the visible page and replaced with a background image of the logo.*

- Subheads *are styled as* <H2> *tags.*

- Body copy *is filled with linked keywords.*

- The concluding link *also contains keywords rather than just "Learn more."*

‹head›
‹title›Graphic Design Classes and Workshops | The MillerWhite School of Design‹/title›

‹meta name="description" content="The MillerWhite School of Design, located in Fairfield County, Connecticut, offers a program for talented high school students interested in exploring the creative and technical aspects of graphic design." /›

‹meta name="keywords" content="art school, norwalk, connecticut, ct, art class, ct art school, graphic design, graphic design school, graphic design program, graphic design class, art workshop, graphic design training, graphic design course, graphic arts class, fairfield county school, brian miller, brian d miller, alex white, alexander white, alexander w white, westport, graphic arts school, summer program, summer camp, summer classes, design degree, graphic design degree, high school activity, art activity, westport art program, ct art school, united states, usa, america, creative workshop, professional development workshop" /›

‹/head›
‹body›

‹!-- Navigation --›
    ‹ul id="nav"›
        ‹li›‹a href="/pre-college"›Pre-College‹/li›
        ‹li›‹a href="/workshops"›Workshops‹/li›
        ‹li›‹a href="/video-library"›Video Library‹/li›
        ‹li›‹a href="/art-colleges"›Art Colleges‹/li›
        ‹li›‹a href="/resources"›Resources‹/li›
        ‹li›‹a href="/online-classes"›Online Classes‹/li›
    ‹/ul›

‹h1›MillerWhite School of Design - Graphic Design Classes, Tutoring and Workshops**‹/h1›**

‹h2›Pre-College Design Classes and Tutoring‹/h2›

‹a href="http://millerwhiteschool.org/about-us"›‹img src="http://millerwhiteschool.org/images/mwsd_logo_black_small.gif" align="left" border="0" title="graphic design for high school" /›‹/a›‹p›The MillerWhite School of Design offers advanced art and ‹a href="graphic-design"›graphic design‹/a› coursework whose purpose is to prepare ‹a href="/students"›students‹/a› for ‹a href="/art-colleges"›professional art education in college‹/a›. ‹/p›

‹p›‹a href="/about-us"›Learn about the design school »‹/a›‹/p›

‹/body›

Internal SEO Factors

On-site SEO influencers can begin with the domain name or URL of the site. Finding the right domain name for a site can be difficult because so many names have already been taken, but choosing a completely arbitrary phrase could hurt a site's SEO value. Using a keyword in the URL can increase its relevance to certain topics. Also, the extension applied to the URL can affect its rank: .com and .org rank higher than other, less popular extensions like .me, .biz, or .us. The age of a domain can also play a role in a site's ranking. Similarly, keyword-rich page addresses can have a positive effect on SEO. For example, instead of naming a blog page using the date (www.example. com/2010/05/05/), the name should reflect the topic (www.example.com/widgets/widget_name/).

Developing a comprehensive SEO strategy means giving each page of a site an identity. This identity is formed and supported by key phrases or terms placed in strategic locations throughout the page. Not all key phrases will be used on every page—in fact, that's a common mistake. Instead, each page should focus on one or two key phrases to provide the most impact for the spiders looking to confirm that a page is what it claims to be. Spiders validate a page by weighing or giving more importance to certain elements over others, making the location of keywords critical to the SEO success of a page.

Probably the most significant location for a key phrase is in the <title> tag for the page. This is the line of text that appears at the top of a user's browser window, above the address bar. Crawl-based search engines place a very high value on this text, as it's very likely to reflect the content of a page. Therefore, the content of the <title> tag should be clear and to the point. Repetitive or non-descriptive <title> tags have a negative effect, such as simply repeating the name of the site on every page title.

GigMasters.com is a site that allows users to book all types of entertainment. Their home page (right) contains text links to many categories of performers. These links combined with other internal SEO techniques consistently put GigMasters.com at the top of search listings.

Ultimately, SEO is about content—valuable content.

Navigation plays a significant role in SEO. Terms that appear in links are given higher value by spiders. Therefore, it's important that the main navigation be styled using "live" text—as opposed to images—when possible. Breadcrumbing, as discussed in chapter 2, "Elements of Usability," is a great way to get keywords into links that appear on every page. Even the links within text play a part in SEO. When leading a user to another page, it's best to include keywords in the link ("Learn more about this widget" instead of just "Learn more"). Text-based site maps provide a useful tool for the user, but they also provide keyword-rich links for spiders. All of these keyword interlinks demonstrate to a search engine that the site, not just a single page, is rich with relevant content.

Ultimately, SEO is about content—valuable content. Each page of a site should contain at least some content; avoid landing pages or splash pages that simply lead a user to another page. (More on landing pages in a bit.) The content of each page should focus on a single key term or phrase and should be updated regularly. Syndicated content, or content that is being pulled from other sites via RSS (Real Simple Syndication), does not have significant SEO value; in fact, it can have a negative effect. Most importantly, content should be interesting to users. Users who value the content of a site generally tell others about it and even link to it from their sites or through social media. These links and high traffic can have a profound effect on the rank of a page.

External SEO Factors

As discussed earlier in this chapter, search engines have shifted their ranking methods away from focusing solely on site content to focusing on a site's popularity. The founders of Google developed this method by studying how college theses are evaluated. If a thesis paper is referenced by another thesis paper, it must have merit, and it must be truly about what the title says it is. The more theses that reference another thesis, the more valuable that thesis must be. Although the methods and details shift over time, that is how Google and similar sites rank Web pages—by the number of sites that link to them. It's a form of validation.

Search engines look at the inbound links (IBL) that a site has—links that people use to connect to a site from other sites. The more inbound links, the more likely it is that a site is trusted. In addition to simply counting the IBLs, spiders read text within the links, and if it matches the content of the page, the ranking is boosted. The greatest value comes from two pages with similar content linking to each other. Similarly, but with a slightly lesser value, outbound links (OBL) to sites with relevant content can help with SEO. These links going out to other sites have lesser value because they can easily be manipulated by a Webmaster. The goal, however, is to demonstrate that the site exists within a community of sites with connections back and forth.

The second way to determine a site's popularity is by evaluating the click-through rate, or the number of times a link has been clicked by a user, on a search engine results page (SERP). This is where the meta description tag for a site comes into play. While Google and other search engines no longer use the content of the metadata to rank a page, they do use the meta description as the blurb below the link on their results pages. A well-written meta description can help entice users to click.

(Opposite) This diagram illustrates the top six external and internal SEO factors. SEO factors shift and change over time, but the goal of a Webmaster is to illustrate to a spider that a site is exactly what it's claiming to be.

A **comprehensive SEO strategy**
targets high-value keywords with
both an internal and external focus.

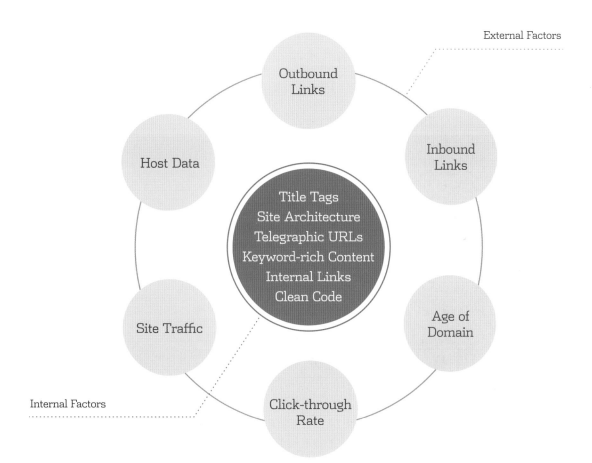

External Factors

Outbound
Links

Host Data

Inbound
Links

Title Tags
Site Architecture
Telegraphic URLs
Keyword-rich Content
Internal Links
Clean Code

Site Traffic

Age of
Domain

Internal Factors

Click-through
Rate

Finally, a site's popularity can be determined by its inclusion
on directory sites. Since directories use knowledgeable human
editors to evaluate the type and quality of content for a site,
getting listed in a directory is a clear indication that a site lives up
to its promise.

Paid Search

The concepts discussed to this point in this chapter produce what are known as organic search results—that is, the ranking of a site happened through the "natural" patterns and habits of users. There's another option to market and promote a site using search engines: paid search. It's called this because Webmasters pay to have their sites listed on the search results page for specific terms. Paid search can be a valuable tool for marketers who are attempting to gain relevance in high-volume markets.

Paid search results appear at the top of most search results pages or on the right-hand side of the page. There is always some indication identifying paid search results, such as "Sponsored Links." This form of advertising can be sharply targeted to a specific segment of users, making it an attractive, relatively low-cost option for many clients. Pricing is usually based on the number of clicks an ad receives; this is why paid search is also called pay per click (PPC). Pricing is also based on the volume of the terms a campaign is targeting (the higher the search volume, the higher the price) as well as the position or "slot" that is desired—the top two slots cost more than the lower slots, for example.

The areas outlined in red are paid or sponsored search results. These links are paid for by advertisers targeting specific keywords—"SEO," in this case.

Paid search advertising can be **sharply targeted** to a specific segment of users, making it an attractive, relatively low-cost option for many clients.

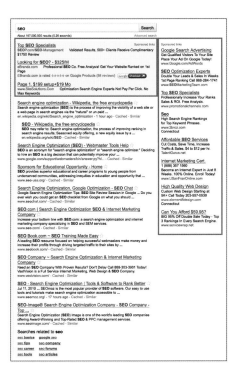

Creating a paid search ad generally involves very little design—certainly none for the ad itself. Instead, ads are copy-based and styled by the advertiser. A paid search ad consists of a headline and body copy that conform to a strict word count. This word count and the need to fit keywords into the text make writing effective paid search ads a unique art form. Copy for an ad also has the ability to be dynamically generated based on a user's search term. For example, a PPC ad campaign for Florida might have a headline that reads, "Looking for vacations in [Keyword]?" When a user searches "Orlando Vacation Packages," the paid search ad would read "Looking for vacations in Orlando?" This gives the user the impression that the content behind this link is extremely relevant to his or her needs.

Paid search ads can link to a page within the advertiser's site, but for greater tracking and conversion, they can also lead to what's called a landing page. Landing pages are specifically designed to maximize the return on investment (ROI) for paid search and advertising campaigns. Often, two or three landing pages will be created to test which messages and design treatments work best. Over time, the pages with lower conversion rates are eliminated, again maximizing the ROI. The topic of converting browsers into buyers is explored further in the next chapter.

CHAPTER 8

MARKETING & CONVERSION

This chapter explores various means of attracting users to a site beyond organic search traffic, converting them into valuable customers, and maintaining a profitable relationship with them. From paid advertising and viral marketing as means to attract visitors, to cross-selling and upselling and email marketing to keep them, each phase of the customer cycle can have a large and lasting effect on the number and value of users that come to a site.

Turning Browsers into Buyers

A Web site needs visitors in order for it to be seen as a success. Previous chapters have examined the methods of driving traffic through search engine optimization (SEO). SEO and search marketing sometimes aren't enough, especially when the client is looking to gain awareness among a specific target demographic for a product or service that's new or that fulfills a need that may not be obvious to a user. In these cases, a more proactive form of marketing is required—Web marketing. Web marketing is a multi–billion-dollar industry covering a wide spectrum of services, from banner advertising and paid sponsorships to more organic forms of advertising like viral and social marketing.

When implemented properly, SEO, combined with effective Web marketing, can drive large volumes of traffic to a site, but sheer numbers alone may not be good enough for a site to succeed long-term. Most sites require the user to take an action, from signing up to be a member, to buying things, to viewing as many pages as possible, to help with advertising impressions. Therefore, it's important that marketing efforts drive high-value visitors to a site. High-value visitors are visitors that come to a Web site not by chance or just to browse, but with the purpose of completing the required action of the site. Finding high-value users is a matter of promoting a site through the proper channels to target the right type of user, and by creating a compelling campaign that appeals to the needs of that target demographic.

Web marketing is a multi-billion-dollar industry covering a wide spectrum of services from banner advertising and paid sponsorships to more organic forms of advertising like viral and social marketing.

Browsers can be converted into high-value visitors, once they arrive at the site, through on-site marketing techniques. Certainly the methods of clear design and planned usability play a role in converting browsers into buyers, but there are other tools that a design team can use to further increase the conversion rate of users. Cross-selling is a means of telling a user, "If you like this, you might like that," and upselling is a means of telling a user, "This product is good, but that product will satisfy more of your needs." Both are effective ways to maximize the value of a user. Sharing mechanisms placed throughout the customer stream on a site can help spread the word about a site through word of mouth. This type of social sharing can be seen as significantly more trustworthy among potential users than banner advertising.

Once a customer has engaged with a client's brand by performing the required action on a site, the next step is to retain that customer. Retaining existing customers is vital for several reasons, but most important is the fact that it costs half as much to retain a customer as it does to attract a new one. Provided that an existing customer is happy with the experience, that person can help attract new customers by telling people about the experience and can even provide valuable feedback to the client about how to enhance the customer experience. Relationship marketing, which is used to communicate with existing customers, includes social marketing and email marketing. These elements help customers feel like they're on the inside and that they're appreciated.

Although entire books can and have been written on any one of these topics, this chapter gives an overview of the considerations a designer must make when attempting to add the most value for a client.

Banner Advertising

Creating an effective banner ad campaign involves many disciplines, from copywriting and design to media strategy, technology, and even psychology. Users have become accustomed to tuning out banner ads, so getting noticed takes knowing the right techniques for a specific audience. As with any form of advertising, Web banner advertising starts with the right media plan. A media plan is a strategy for determining where and when the banners will appear. These choices are made with several factors in mind, including the relevancy of the content on a site compared to the advertisement, the amount of traffic a site has, and the cost per click that a site offers.

Once in place, a media plan will dictate the types and sizes of interactive marketing units (IMU) needed for a campaign. The Interactive Advertising Bureau (IAB) has set standards for file size, dimension, and animation time. Included in the IAB standards are Universal Ad Package (UAP) sizes. UAP standards make it easier for companies to advertise, since advertisers only need to create a finite set of banner sizes that can be used across a wide range of sites. Universal Ad Package sizes (in pixels) include:

Leaderboard	728 x 90
Wide Skyscraper	160 x 600
Medium rectangle	300 x 250
Rectangle	180 x 150
Mobile Leaderboard	320 x 50

A diagram showing the complete set of IAB IMUs is featured on the next spread.

IAB Ad Dimensions, File Sizes, and Animation Limits

Micro Bar
88 x 31, 10K, :15

Pop-Under
720 x 300, 40K, :15

Button 1
120 x 90, 20K, :15

Leaderboard
728 x 90, 40K, :15

Button 2
120 x 60, 20K, :15

Full Banner
468 x 60, 40K, :15

Half Banner
234 x 60, 30K, :15

Vertical Rectangle
240 x 400, 40K, :15

Square Pop-Up
250 x 250, 40K, :15

3:1 Rectangle
300 x 100, 40K, :15

Half-Page Ad
300 x 600, 40K, :15

Wide Skyscraper
160 x 600, 40K, :15

Skyscraper
120 x 600, 40K, :15

Vertical Banner
120 x 240, 30K, :15

Square Button
125 x 125, 30K, :15

Large Rectangle
336 x 280, 40K, :15

Medium Rectangle
300 x 250, 40K, :15

Rectangle
180 x 150, 40K, :15

A **click-through rate** is the number of people who have clicked on the banner and is expressed as a percentage of the number of people who have seen the ad, called **impressions**.

When creating a banner ad, a designer is looking to generate a high click-through rate. A click-through rate is the number of people who have clicked on the banner to go to the client's site. The click-through rate is expressed as a percentage of the number of people who have seen the ad, called impressions. For example, if a banner is on a page where 25,000 people visit and 250 people click the banner, the click-through rate is one percent—an admirable rate for a site with this amount of traffic. This level of detailed statistical data is unique to Web marketing, and it enables a high level of control over a campaign. Often, a banner campaign will involve multiple versions of a banner and over time, high-performing banners can replace low-performing banners to maximize the click-through rate of each placement.

Banners present a unique design challenge because they usually exist in a cluttered environment. These banners for the Starbucks Love campaign are instantly recognizable across different sites and the design is consistent throughout the varying UAP sizes.

Detach and Distribute

Because click-through rates are often a very small percentage of the overall impressions a banner receives, marketers have begun thinking about and utilizing the space within a banner differently. A technique called detach and distribute brings critical content and site features to the banner space, allowing users to engage with a brand without ever leaving the page they're on. Pioneered by Tom Beeby, creative director at the interactive marketing firm Beeby, Clark and Meyler, detach and distribute employs rich media to display a video, capture email addresses, or allow real-time social interactions, for example. This tactic of creating a mini-site within a site can be highly effective for increasing awareness of a product or service.

These banners created for GE display both pre-recorded and live video content from GE.com and allow users to comment on the them in real time, right within the banner space.

Contextually relevant ads are ads that respond directly to the environment in which they are served.

Context is a critical aspect of all forms of advertising, but with Web advertising it can be taken to an even higher level. Contextually relevant ads are ads that respond directly to the environment in which they are served. This can mean something simple like placing an ad for fishing boats on a fishing Web site, but it can also be much more specific by drawing on data from the user, including time-specific or location-specific placements. Contextually relevant banners have been shown to be significantly more effective than one-size-fits-all banner campaigns.

Because of their unusual dimensions, shapes, file size limitations, and the need for immediate communication of a message, banner ads present a significant design challenge. The best advice a designer can heed is to put him- or herself in the shoes of the user and ask, "What would I respond to?" The answer is almost always a simple, relevant message, clearly stated, with an obvious call to action. Animation can help grab attention and/or build a message within a limited space, but most sites do not permit repeating or looping animation, since it can be very distracting to a user. Thus, the final frame of the banner should be designed and written in a way that all the critical information appears. The call to action, which is a sentence with a verb (learn, click, try, etc.) inviting the user to do something, should be clear—perhaps encased in a button-like object—and should directly relate to the content of the page the user is taken to after clicking the banner.

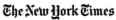

These banners from Apple Computer seem like ordinary ad placements, but there's a twist—the banners are synced with one another, making it possible for them to work together. In the ad seen here, Mac and PC are reacting to the leaderboard banner, which states that Apple is number one in customer experience, while the men in the seemingly unrelated "hair replacement" ad chime in to the conversation.

These amusing and engaging ads were awarded a Webby, one of the highest honors an online campaign can receive.

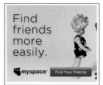

These ads for MySpace (top) and Pringles (left) use humor to engage the user and convey a brand message. This Pringles ad has received multiple accolades for its innovative use of adverting space. The ad continues seemingly forever with mundane conversation as part of Pringles' "Over-Sharing" campaign.

Getting a user to engage with a
banner ad means getting a user to
engage with a client's brand.

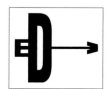

(Above) This single banner for Zippo lighters appears to be two banners, where the gentleman in the upper banner is being heated up by the lighter in the lower banner.

(Left) These banners for the Toyota Prius invite users to draw on the banner. This action triggers an animation that explains a feature of the car.

This interactive banner from Lotus Notes collaboration software invited users to collaborate by manipulating the letters of the word "IDEA" into various pictographs. Each user interacting with the ad would be responsible for shaping a single letter.

Rich media banners can be effective in grabbing a user's attention, but they can also be costly to produce and place, making them suitable for a limited number of clients.

In addition to standard ad units, there are third-party solutions, such as EyeWonder and EyeBlaster (Media Mind), which provide a variety of rich-media expandable banners. These banners include a wide range of interactive experiences, from a simple expanding banner, to banners that communicate with one another, to page takeovers or roadblocks where the entire Web page is consumed with an ad. These banners can be effective in grabbing a user's attention, but they can also be costly to produce and place—so they're most suitable to a small number of clients who have large online advertising budgets.

These rich media banners for McDonald's completely take over the Web page. The top image is known as a "peel-back" ad, where the page can be turned like a page of a book to reveal an advertising message. The bottom ad is an expandable banner featuring characters that dance across the screen.

(Top) This ad for Tostitos includes two standard placements, a leaderboard, and big box, and also the background "skin," which visually relates to the ads.

(Bottom left) This ad for Sony features an expandable video player. The player expands over the page content, making the video larger.

(Bottom right) This video game ad consists of a leaderboard that expands with a graphic and a video, as well as the big box ad along the right side.

Viral Marketing

Viral marketing gets its name from the way a virus spreads rapidly and "infects" a population organically. Viral marketing works because such pieces provide some sort of entertainment value beyond the thousands of ordinary advertising messages consumers are bombarded with on a daily basis. Successful viral pieces hit on a universal concept—humor, fear, sex—and at first may not appear to be marketing pieces at all. Branding is usually subtle, or in some cases nonexistent. Because consumers are so overloaded with advertising messages, they're also very suspicious, which makes viral marketing difficult—very difficult, in fact.

Elf Yourself from OfficeMax allowed users to place family members' faces on dancing elves.

If a piece of marketing "goes viral," the impact can be profound. An early example of successful viral marketing was for the film *The Blair Witch Project*. Instead of standard big-budget TV and print ads, the producers released short clips of the film on the Internet. The clips were hauntingly scary, and the supporting

Web site blurred the lines between what was real and what was part of the movie. The film cost $350,000 to create and market, but grossed nearly $250 million at the box office—the highest profit-to-cost ratio of any film in history.

Have a break, have a Jesus Kit-Kat

Easter is time for Easter Bunny potato chips and Jesus sightings, and the latest is a doozy: Jesus has been spotted in a Kit-Kat.

The Kit-Kat hails from the Netherlands, where the story is a little Google Translate sketchy. Here's what I managed to pull out (original link/ translated)

Viral marketing doesn't have to be high-tech or high budget. This viral campaign from Kit Kat started with a photo and an email about seeing the face of Jesus. It quickly spread around the Internet, carrying with it the Kit-Kat messaging.

The phrase "viral marketing" may be relatively new, but the concept isn't. Guerilla marketing, popular in the 1990s, involved tactics such as spray-painting company logos, as if by street artists, to get people talking and to gain credibility among an urban demographic. Even political propaganda or rumor-spreading can be considered a form of viral marketing.

Burger King and their interactive agency Crispin, Porter + Bogusky have a long history of creating viral content. Seen here is the subservient chicken who would do anything (really anything) the user typed into the field. Also seen here is The Simpsons Movie *tie-in,* Simpsonize Yourself. *This Flash application allowed users to create Simpsons versions of themselves.*

Brief History of Viral Videos

2000
JOHN WEST SALMON

One of the earliest viral videos was this amusing TV spot for John West Salmon. Styled like a nature documentary complete with narration, the video quickly turns into an outrageous kung fu fight between a fisherman and a bear.

2001
BMW FILMS

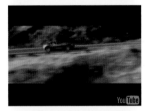

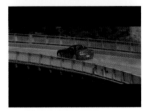

Traditionally, companies try to have their products placed in high-budget films. In this example, BMW placed a high-budget film in their advertising. This glossy series of viral films was directed by David Fincher and Guy Richie and starred actors such as Don Cheadle, Clive Owen, and even Madonna.

2002
AGENT PROVOCATEUR

This over-the-top viral video features Australian actress and singer Kylie Minogue riding a mechanical bull in Agent Provocateur lingerie. What started as a Super Bowl ad became a wildly popular Web video—especially among the male audience.

2006
DOVE

As part of Dove's "Real Beauty" campaign, this viral video titled "Evolution" looks at the transformation of a model from makeup to lighting to retouching using time-lapse photography. The message to young women was as powerful as the visual.

2006
HERE IT GOES AGAIN

Take six treadmills, four hipster musicians, and one infectious song and get this low-budget, ingenious, and fun viral video. This video is proof that viral marketing is more about ideas than big budgets.

2007
GUITARMASTERPRO.NET

This extremely unassuming video featuring a 21-year-old guitar player playing Pachelbel's Canon received over 60 million views on YouTube. The video for a guitar lesson site relied completely on the talent of the subject—and it worked.

Social Marketing

Social marketing is similar to viral marketing in that it spreads organically through word of mouth—but social marketing usually involves a direct benefit to the user. Think of it this way: Viral marketing is a person going to a party with a cold and spreading it to the other partygoers; social marketing is a person going to a party with good news and actively telling as many people as he or she can.

Social marketing is used as much to get new customers as it is to retain existing customers. Building a social relationship with a customer by inviting them to like a page on Facebook, for example, enables client organizations to market to these consumers in a new way. Offering coupons or exclusive deals can make consumers feel as if they're part of a brand and therefore will be more likely to spread positive information about a brand to their social networks. These types of seemingly unaided endorsements have a profound ability to influence consumer opinion—so much so that companies are continually trying to blur the lines between "friends" and brands.

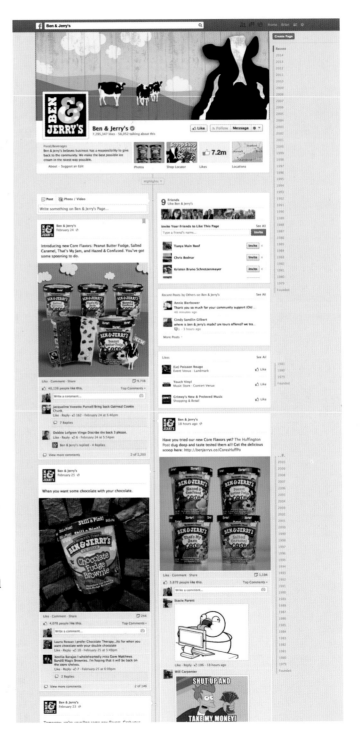

Social media isn't about fancy design; it's about engaging consumers on a different level than other forms of marketing. Social marketing is a conversation with the customer that makes the customer feel welcome and part of the client's company, as these examples illustrate.

Ben and Jerry's and JetBlue, whose Facebook and Twitter pages are seen here, respectively, do an excellent job extending their brand images with social media. This is in part because these brands already had a conversational relationship with their customers.

Pinterest.com has emerged as an engaging social media tool that companies are using to promote and grow their businesses.
The visual nature of Pinterest allows users or potential customers to scan a lot of information very quickly.

Viral marketing is a person going to a party with a cold and spreading it to the other partygoers; **social marketing** is a person going to a party with good news and actively telling as many people as he or she can.

Perhaps the most famous and certainly one of the earliest social/viral campaigns was this one from Burger King. The Whopper Sacrifice called upon Facebook users to "sacrifice" a few of their friends for a free hamburger. The campaign was extremely successful; however, it violated a rule on Facebook that bans telling friends when they've been defriended. Because of this, the campaign was ended but its impact lives on.

Getting a user to take action involves the right products, promotion, pricing, and placement—**the four P's of marketing**.

On-Site Marketing

Once a user has found a site, it's important to the client that the value is maximized. Clients want to get the most out of each visitor, and this can mean different things for different sites—from becoming a member to filling a shopping cart with products to buy. Getting a user to take this action can take more than clear navigation, well-planned usability, and effective design; as discussed in previous chapters, it also involves the right products, promotion, pricing, and placement—the four P's of marketing.

Having the right product development and pricing strategy is largely the responsibility of the client and is usually determined prior to starting a Web project. Promoting and placing these products, however, can be the job of the Web project team. Promotion is a means of giving information about a product that piques the interest of the user. It's the job of an effective marketer to highlight important features of a product or service and clearly differentiate it from the competition. The Web offers a variety of ways to promote a product or service, from photo galleries and slideshows to highly interactive product showcases.

The product display on MarieCatribs.com is not only user friendly but client friendly as well. The photography and clean layout make accessing the products easy and inviting, which can lead to more sales and higher profits for the client.

JaqkCellars.com does a magnificent job displaying their products in a way that enhances their appeal. The product pages are simple, with a single focal point: the product. Flash is used to provide a 360-degree spinning view of the bottle. The dark "ADD TO CART" buttons stand out from the page, making it easy for the user to enter the buying process.

To **cross-sell** is to recommend other products to a user based on his or her interest in a particular item.

The other P of on-site marketing is placement, which gives the user access to the product outside the context of the standard product or catalog page. Placement is the association of a product or service to content or other products or services. On a site that has health information and also sells health products, for example, an article about sprained ankles might be accompanied by a product placement of ankle braces for sale in the store.

Cross-selling is a form of placement. Online retailers understand that if a user is in the mood to buy one item, he or she is more easily persuaded to purchase more items. This is where cross-selling comes in. To cross-sell is to recommend other products to a user based on his or her interest in a particular item. Cross-selling associations can be done one of two ways: by the client linking products that relate to each other functionally—e.g., if you buy this Apple computer you might want this Apple mouse—or with purchase history, where users make the associations with their buying patterns—e.g., "Users who bought this item also bought…" Upselling is similar to cross-selling, except the goal is to get the customer to buy more expensive items or services. An effective way to upsell is through the use of a features chart. Features charts show side-by-side comparisons of one product to another, highlighting the benefits of purchasing the higher-priced item.

The items along the left side of this page from MeAndMommyToBe.com are related to the main product in some way and likely to be purchased at the same time.

Both TommyBahama.com and JPeterman.com cross-sell their garments by offering additional items of a similar style on the product pages.

PotteryBarn.com offers a variety of selling tools on their product pages—from items in a set and related items to customer ratings and reviews.

&c.

ORIGINAL ETCETERA ART

Email Marketing

The site has been found and the sale made, but the customer cycle has one more component to close the loop: relationship building. Building a relationship with a user-turned-customer by regularly communicating with the person can be extremely valuable to a client. Repeat customers not only cost less than new customers, but they are likely to tell their friends about the product or service, which breeds new customers. One of the most effective ways to maintain a relationship with a customer is through email marketing. Email marketing "pushes" information about the client's product or service to the customer. Relationship marketing can take the form of a newsletter, where product information is accompanied by information that's valuable to the user.

TWELVE HAND-PAINTED PIECES
BY SARGIO SIGNS

There are strict laws governing the use of email marketing that designers and their clients should be aware of. Failure to comply with the laws contained in the CAN-SPAM Act can bring stiff fines to a client. The CAN-SPAM Act dictates the following guidelines for email marketing:

FRAMED IN RECLAIMED BARNBOARD

- Don't use false or misleading header information ("From," "Reply to")
- Don't use deceptive subject lines
- Identify the message as an ad
- Tell recipients where you're located
- Tell recipients how to opt out of receiving future emails
- Honor opt-out requests promptly
- Monitor what others are doing on your behalf

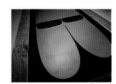

PAINTED WITH ONE-SHOT LETTERING ENAMEL

VISIT THE 1151 GALLERY OR SHOP ONLINE

Source: http://www.business.ftc.gov/documents/bus61-can-spam-act-compliance-guide-business

Photoshop CC

Download a free trial of the fastest, most responsive Photoshop yet and repurpose assets across Photoshop documents with linked Smart Objects. And experience Perspective Warp, the new feature that lets you change the viewpoint of a photo after it's been shot.

Get started

Illustrator CC

Finesse your designs more directly and intuitively with Live Corners. Round, invert, or chamfer one or multiple corners at the same time.

Get started

InDesign CC

Access the library of over 700 Typekit desktop fonts directly from the InDesign font menu (for complete membership only). The new missing font workflow even notes missing fonts in your documents, locates them in Typekit, and prompts you to sync them to your computer with a single click.

Get started

Adobe Muse CC

Create and publish dynamic websites for desktop and mobile devices — without writing code. Design using intuitive tools and add interactivity like scrolling effects, slide shows, contact forms, and videos.

Get started

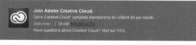

These email templates from House Industries (left) and Adobe Systems (right) illustrate a simple elegance that's required for email designs. Because of the restrictions of mail browsers to display HTML and the need for immediate communication, email templates must focus on simplicity and clear hierarchy.

The **subject line** of an email acts as a headline and can play a pivotal role in the success of an email campaign.

Designing an email template presents another set of unique design challenges for Web designers. This is because email clients (Outlook, Mac Mail, etc.) are far less sophisticated in their ability to display HTML than Web browsers are. For example, the standard width of an email is 600 pixels, as opposed to 990 for a Web site. File sizes matter, since the user hasn't necessarily requested to see the content of the email. Emails with long load times tend to get deleted and go unread. Emails are primarily limited to HTML and standard image formats—jpg, gif—but Flash, JavaScript, and movie formats are currently unsupported by most email clients. Linking to external files for styling, for example, is also unsupported. Therefore CSS coding must be done "in-line," meaning in the individual tags for each HTML element.

The subject line of an email acts as a headline and can play a pivotal role in the success of an email. Subject lines should speak specifically to the subject of the email with clarity and brevity. Often, as with online banner advertising, multiple subject lines are tested for efficacy, and subject lines with higher open rates can replace more poorly performing lines to maximize the success of an email. Email layouts require simplicity even more so than Web pages because they are often scanned by the user. When creating an email, a designer should consider the primary goal of the email and focus the design on that element by creating a clear hierarchy of information. Emails should include at least some HTML-based text because some email clients and mobile devices only display the text of an email. The footer of an email, by law, needs to indicate who the email was sent to, who it was sent by, and a means for the user to opt out from receiving future emails.

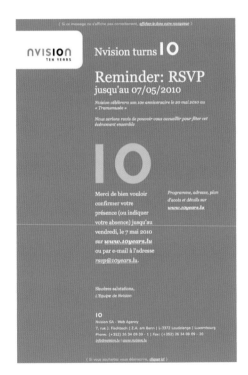

These email templates illustrate how, even within the constraints of email browsers, the design can still be an extension of a client's brand, increasing brand recognition among users.

Scott & Nix Forward to a Friend

Newsletter
Fishing with Kids
May 2011

Take a Child Fishing

THE SUNFISH

Tips for a successful first outing with your young angler

1. Keep the trip short. **2.** Catch a fish.

3. Have a sandwich and a juice box on hand for when the fishing's done.

Pick a warm day, and take your youngster to a dock on a pond or a lake for sunfish. Beginnings are a delicate thing, and no one likes to get skunked, especially kids.

Trout and bass can be finicky and elusive. Sunfish are eager feeders and plentiful in most freshwater lakes.

Feel free to share our newsletter with your friends. Click here to forward it to someone you know.

The Quarry

It's nice to know what you're catching and sunfishes are an amazingly diverse group. All are members of the large Centrarchidae family, which includes freshwater basses, crappies, bluegill, pumpkinseed, and others. In all, there are 27 species and all are native to North America. The classic group of sunfishes, a.k.a. panfishes, are all included on the Sunfishes of North America wall poster.

SUNFISHES OF NORTH AMERICA

SPECIES INCLUDE:

pumpkinseed	redear sunfish	flier
bluegill	dollar sunfish	shadow bass
spotted sunfish	warmouth	Ozark bass
orangespotted sunfish	redbreast sunfish	black crappie
redspotted sunfish	green sunfish	white crappie
longear sunfish	rock bass	

The Sunfish of North America poster is illustrated by the amazing Joe Tomelleri. You can see more of his illustrations on posters or our site, and at his website, americanfishes.com.

The Gear

The Pole

Any light-weight fishing pole will do with a small reel and some 2- to 4-pound test line. You don't even really need a reel. This might be the time to use that old cane pole in the garage or to cut a branch from a willow and make one yourself.

The Bobber

A simple one-inch adjustable bobber will do the trick. Place the bobber 18 inches above the hook.

The Hook and Knot

Use a number 6 hook, tied on the line using a clinch knot:

The Bait

Earthworms (cut in small portions) are the traditional bait. You can also use live crickets (easy to catch in the cool of the morning), bits of soft pet food, small balls of white bread, mealworms, or even uncooked bacon. Sunnies will bite at just about anything.

Catching sunnies couldn't be easier and along the way, you can patiently explain some safety rules about hooks and how to gently release the fish back into the water. You will be rewarded with a very happy child and perhaps even the beginnings of a life-long angler.

The Technique

Toss the baited hook and bobber toward the shore or near the protective cover of the dock. Let it splash down and wait three seconds (counting it out with your child). Reel or pull the bobber back toward you, 12 inches, and let it sit. Keep an eye on it. It won't take long for the nibbling to begin. When the bobber goes under, give a slight tug to set the hook, and then slowly reel it in. Don't yank too hard, lest your child be unceremoniously introduced to a flying fish! If the bobber is just bobbing and not going under, try a smaller bit of bait.

Fish Stories

Before you get home, be sure to work out your story together. How big was the fish? How many did you catch? Fish stories are an integral part of the experience, and while we don't advocate fibbing, a little hyperbole won't hurt.

—Scott & Nix

Forward to a Friend   Subscribe to Our Newsletter   Contact Us

CHAPTER 9

ANALYSIS

The final component of the Web design cycle is analysis. While all forms of marketing are analyzed and optimized, no form of marketing or design can be analyzed with the immediacy, accuracy, and depth that Web marketing can. What used to take weeks or months to collect and report now happens in real time. This immediacy allows marketers and designers to make calculated adjustments that improve the overall performance of their online assets. From banner campaigns, to site design and usability, to email campaigns and social media, all aspects of user activity and brand engagement can be tracked at a granular level.

Closing the Loop

Web site statistics have come a long way from the counters that used to be seen at the bottom of Web pages. Those could only tell the Webmaster the number of people who visited the site. Today, almost any action by a user can be tracked and analyzed—from where the visitor came; what words were used to search and find a site; how long the visitor was on a site; how many pages were visited—right down to if the person converted into a paying customer. Beyond the behavioral statistics, demographic information such as geographic location, browser type, OS, and connection speed can also be collected. Such statistics provide a marketing and design team with a wealth of useful information for optimizing site and campaign performance.

Analytical data can help remove a level of subjectivity from the creative process by providing qualitative data that supports one direction over another. Unfortunately, this data may not always support the designer's position. Web designers must be open to the notion that their designs will need to change and shift based on the habits and feedback of their users. What works for an audience today may be different next year, next month, or even next week. Technology evolves, users evolve, and environments evolve, making the Web and Web design more about progress and adaptability than permanence or even the level of perfection that comes with other forms of design.

The most common method of collecting statistical data is with Google Analytics, a free yet remarkably robust tracking system provided by Google.com. There are other free services, such as Piwik, which is a PHP-based open source system with many of the same features as Google Analytics. There are paid services, like WebTrends, that help their clients interpret their site statistics with reports and consulting.

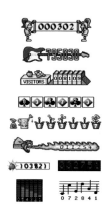

These counter icons are what Webmasters once used to track users who came to a site.

Analysis

257

In the case of Web design, very often **progress** is more important than **perfection.**

This chapter examines various data points that Google Analytics reports on and how they can affect the decisions a designer makes. Each data point can provide valuable information, but the full potential of Web analysis comes when the statistics are used in concert with one another. Focusing too heavily on any single statistic can mislead a designer. Combining key statistics can give a more complete picture of the strengths and weaknesses of a site. For example, if a site has a low average time-on-site statistic, this can be either a positive or a negative— but it's difficult to tell with this statistic alone. If the low average time on site is combined with a high bounce rate (the percentage of people who leave after only viewing the home page), then there could be an issue with engaging people in the site content. If, however, the low average time-on-site statistic is combined with a high number of pages viewed and the exit page leads a user to an online retailer to buy the product, for example, this would mean the site is working quite effectively in driving users to purchase.

What follows are brief explanations of various key statistics that Google Analytics reports on.

This is the Visitors Overview page of Google Analytics. By carefully tracking and cross-referencing the information displayed here, a designer can learn critical information about the habits of the users of a site and possibly inform future design decisions.

User Data

These data points tell a Webmaster or designer what he or she needs to know about the users who visit a site. From the number of visits to the capabilities of the user's technology, understanding the user is critical to the success of a Web site project.

VISITS

This indicates the total number of visitors to a site. It includes new and returning visitors and is an indication of the success or failure of an SEO strategy or marketing campaign. The number of visits can be an overrated statistic in that it's not an indication of the value of the visitors in terms of how long they spent on the site or what percentage are returning because they liked the experience. Like most of the statistics in this chapter, the analyst needs to cross-reference the visits statistic with other statistics to really understand its value.

The term *visits* is sometimes confused with *hits*, but the two terms are not synonymous. A hit is a reference to the retrieval of a page asset from a server. For example, if a single user goes to a page with eight images and an external CSS file, each image plus the page and the CSS file will count as a hit—in this case, ten hits—but the page will have gotten only one visit. While hits have importance to an IT staff, designers and marketers should avoid citing hits as an indicator of a site's popularity, as it can represent a misleading and inflated view of site statistics.

ABSOLUTE UNIQUE VISITORS

Absolute unique visitors are visitors visiting a site for the very first time. Analytical reporting takes place over a specific time period. The default in Google Analytics is the past thirty days, but the range can be set for any length of time. Absolute unique visitors are not only visiting a site for the first time during the selected time period, they are visiting the site for the first time ever. This can be helpful in understanding the success of a marketing campaign whose goal is to build awareness among a new target audience.

NEW VISITS

New Versus Returning Visits is sometime confused with absolute unique visitors, but there's a slight difference. New visits are visits to a site by users who have visited the site prior to the time range being analyzed, but it's their first time back during that time period. This data point is expressed as a percentage—56% indicates 56 percent of the visitors were new during the time period, and by inference, for example, 44 percent had visited the site more than once during the time period.

The image above shows the map overlay feature in Google Analytics. The darker the green, the more visitors that have come to a site from that country.

BROWSER CAPABILITIES

The Browser Capabilities statistic shows both the number and percentage of browser types and technologies used by the visitors of a site. Understanding the capabilities of the majority of the users of a site is essential for designing and building the right experience for them. Included under browser capabilities is not only the browser type (Safari, Firefox, Internet Explorer, Chrome, etc.) but also the operating system, screen resolution and colors, Flash version, and Java support. Each of these points paints a picture of the target users' capabilities and informs decisions made surrounding the types of technology used for a Web site.

NETWORK PROPERTIES

This feature indicates the service providers and hostnames of the users, but the most relevant data point for designers is the connection speed. Common connection speeds include (from fastest to slowest) T1, DSL, cable, ISDN, and dialup. Knowing the connection speed of the majority of the users of a site is critical to designing the right experience. The slower the connection speed, the lower the tolerance will likely be for graphics, imagery, and media assets that take time to download.

MOBILE

Increasingly, sites are being viewed using mobile devices, such as iPhones. This section of Google Analytics displays both the devices and the carriers of a site's mobile users. If a large number of visitors frequent a site via mobile devices, it may warrant a mobile version of the site.

MAP OVERLAY

Understanding the geographic location of the visitors to a site is can play a role in informing the direction of a site. The Map Overlay feature of Google Analytics shows the countries where users have visited a site.

The intensity of the color indicates the number of visitors—the darker the green, the more visitors. This allows Web content developers to gear the content of a site in a way that is relevant to the users in the countries visiting the site.

LANGUAGES

Similar to the map overlay, the Languages report can help a client understand the needs of the actual demographic, which can be different from the target demographic. Languages are determined by the users' computer preferences and are reported in Google Analytics.

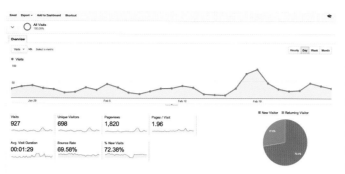

This visual shows the traffic source information. The pie chart indicates the three types of traffic sources: direct traffic, referring sites, and search engines.

Source Data

Once there's an understanding of the user, it's important to know how the user is finding a site. Source data plays a critical role in search engine optimization as well as marketing, because it gives a Webmaster the knowledge of how users may have become aware of a site.

TRAFFIC SOURCES

Understanding the source of the visitor traffic to a site is critical for optimizing SEO and marketing efforts. Google Analytics' All Traffic Sources report shows the sources of traffic, including direct, search engines, and referring sites. The direct traffic number indicates users who simply typed the URL into their Web browsers. This can indicate a number of things to a marketing team, including whether the user saw a Web address in a non-online advertising campaign like print, radio, or TV.

REFERRING SITES

The Referring Sites tab shows sites that visitors used to link to the site being analyzed. This data is extremely valuable from an SEO perspective. The more sites that link to the subject site, the higher that site will rank for certain terms. Google Analytics displays the referring sites and the number of visitors that came from that site. By clicking on a site in the list, one can see the specific page the link came from.

SEARCH ENGINES

The Search Engine report shows the search engines that visitors used to search and find the subject site. This report can play an important role in determining the right sites for a search marketing campaign, as marketers want to advertise in the places where their target audience will see them.

KEYWORDS

The Keywords report is one of the most essential tools for understanding how users are finding a site. It shows a list of the words that visitors used to search for and link to a site. This can help validate or disprove an SEO key term strategy by showing the project team what words are actually being used to find a site. If the report matches the list of keywords the site targeted, the SEO strategy is a success. If they don't match, however, one of two things must occur. The team could look at the list and adjust it if there's an indication that the list misjudged what users were after. More likely, the implementation of the SEO tactics could be reexamined and improvements made to increase the performance of the original keyword list.

The content overview page on Google Analytics, pictured above, shows the pageviews, unique views, and bounce rates for a site.

Content Data

The final step in understanding analytical data is looking at what users are doing on a site. When combined, stats like landing pages, time on site, pageviews, and exit pages can give a clear view of how users are using a site.

PAGEVIEWS

Pageviews is as simple as the name implies—the number of pages viewed by visitors to a site. Pageviews is a broad statistic and, like total visits, can be somewhat misleading. For example, if a user reloads a page, that can count as a second pageview. Similarly, if a user browses from a page to another page, then back to the original, that too will count as two pageviews for the original page.

AVERAGE PAGEVIEWS

Average Pageviews is the result of the number of pageviews divided by the number of visits on a given day. This can be helpful in showing trends from day to day. Whereas Pageviews refers to the total number of pages viewed over the entire time period, Average Pageviews refers to the number of pages the average visitor viewed on a single day, which is then tracked over time.

BOUNCE RATE

The Bounce Rate is usually given as a percentage and indicates the percentage of people who left a site after visiting only a single landing page—the home page, for example. Generally, a high bounce rate is not a good thing. It can indicate that information is difficult to navigate, the traffic sources are misleading, or the content is of poor quality. In some rare cases, a high bounce rate is acceptable. For example, if a landing page effectively targets a specific keyword, a user may arrive at the page, get all the information needed, and then perhaps leave by clicking on a banner ad placed on the page. Despite going to only one page, that user might have a favorable opinion of the site and the client-generated revenue with the ad click. More often, however, a high bounce rate is not good.

The Entrance Path *feature of Google Analytics shows where users entered a site and, based on that entry point, where they ended up.*

AVERAGE TIME ON SITE

Average Time On Site is, as the name implies, the average length of time users spend on a site. This statistic is calculated by subtracting the difference in time between the first and last pageview. As a result, it can be somewhat inaccurate in terms of the exact amount of time users are spending on a site. If the last page of the visit involves a time-consuming task—which is usually the case if a user is watching a video or reading an article— then the time on site would actually be much longer. Designers and Webmasters are looking for trends, rather than specific time, when analyzing the time-on-site statistics.

TOP LANDING PAGES

The Top Landing Pages are the pages that visitors are using to enter a site. Therefore, this data can be critical to a designer's decision-making process. It's important for designers to understand that not all visitors will be "landing" or arriving at the home page. With SEO and referring links, almost any page of the site can be a landing page. Designers need to provide the same type of marketing, usability, and accessibility on landing pages as they do on the home page.

TOP CONTENT

Top Content shows the pages on a site that were most viewed by visitors. This statistic shows the specific pages that were viewed and how many times they were viewed. This report also displays the average time users spent on each page, the bounce rate for each page, and the percentage of users who exited on a specific page. This can be helpful in gaining an understanding of what users want from a site. It can also help to show prospective advertisers where users are spending the most time when planning advertising sales.

TOP EXIT PAGES

Exit Pages are the last pages users viewed on a site. Users exit a site for various reasons—they've completed their task, or they clicked on an ad or link—or for less positive reasons, like they couldn't find what they were looking for or couldn't complete the required task. Together with landing pages and content statistics, exit page statistics complete the picture of how users arrive, what they do, and how they leave a site. Pages with unexpectedly high exit rates should be reexamined by the design team for usability issues that could cause users to leave the site prematurely.

INDEX